FURTHER C

WALKS FOR M

James F. Edwards

30 Walks with sketch maps

COUNTRYSIDE BOOKS
NEWBURY, BERKSHIRE

Countryside Books' walking guides cover most areas of England and Wales and include the following series:

County Rambles
Walks for Motorists
Exploring Long Distance Paths
Literary Walks
Pub Walks

A complete list is available from the publishers.

First published 1981
by Frederick Warne Ltd.

This completely revised and updated edition
published 1992
© James F. Edwards 1992

COUNTRYSIDE BOOKS
3, Catherine Road
Newbury, Berkshire

ISBN 1 85306 169 7
Sketch Maps by the Author

Cover photograph: View from Alderley Edge
taken by Bill Meadows

Typeset by Acorn Bookwork, Salisbury, Wiltshire
Produced through MRM Associates Ltd., Reading
Printed in England by J.W. Arrowsmith Ltd., Bristol

For Jackie

Acknowledgements

Thanks are due to the staff of The Public Rights of Way Unit, Commerce House, Chester, and in particular Messrs. G. E. Porter and M. J. Nutkins, for their helpful advice and invaluable assistance with route checking.

Contents

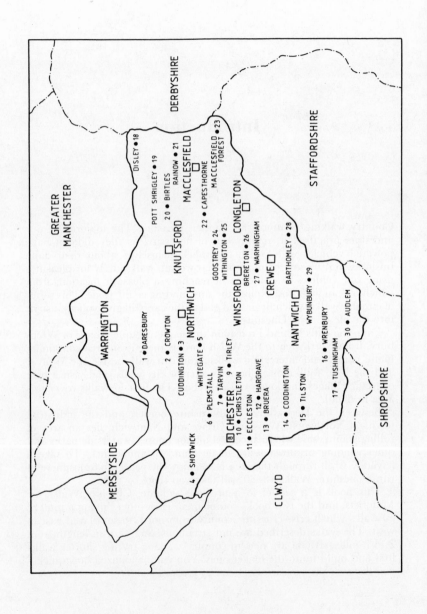

Introduction

Country walking is almost a forgotten pleasure. The majority of our ancestors practised it, mainly out of necessity, as they did not have powered vehicles with which to propel themselves about their daily business. But we are fortunate in that we can walk purely for pleasure, using our vehicles as a means of reaching a pleasant location, from which we can walk and explore the surrounding countryside. This series of circular walks which begin and end at the car, will give you an insight into the life of rural Cheshire.

From the cliffs behind Frodsham to the picturesque village of Wrenbury, from Northwich to the Welsh border, there is an area containing many varied and interesting walks. You can walk beside the Weaver and the Dee, walk along Chester's ancient city walls, and visit a host of scenic villages and lovely old churches. The first 17 walks cover this area in detail.

Between the Derbyshire—Staffordshire border, and the industrial towns of Northwich, Winsford, Crewe and Nantwich, lies an area of rolling countryside where ancestral manor houses, waterside paths and quiet winding bridleways are to be found in abundance. To take a leisurely stroll through the area is to enjoy the peaceful atmosphere of rural Cheshire. Walks 18–30 will take you there.

This book is a sequel to a previous volume, Cheshire Walks for Motorists, and the two books complement each other, giving a total of 60 walks which criss-cross the county from north to south and east to west. The walks described are not strenuous, and vary in length from 2 to 8 miles. If you are new to country walking try the shorter walks first and build up to the longer ones. You will be amazed how quickly you discover the pleasures of country walking.

Rights of Way

All the routes described are on public rights of way, but footpaths can be legally re-routed due to land development or road alterations, in which case diversionary signs are usually shown by the Highway Authority.

If a right of way is obstructed, it would be helpful if details of the obstruction, together with its location, are reported to:

The Public Rights of Way Unit
Cheshire County Council
Commerce House
Hunter Street
Chester
CH1 2QP

Equipment

Footwear is all important. Waterproof walking shoes or boots are recommended, preferably worn over woollen socks. Smooth soled shoes should not be worn as they can cause accidents and make walking hard work, especially after wet weather.

Lightweight waterproof clothing should always be carried to combat the variable English weather.

A small rucksack can be useful to carry such items as food, cameras, binoculars and the like, which help to make a walk that much more enjoyable.

A note regarding maps and map references

The Ordnance Survey maps referred to at the beginning of each walk are the 1:50,000 Landranger Series. Four of these maps cover all the territory of the walks described in this book; these being maps 108, 109, 117 and 118.

Although you should not encounter problems in finding where to park the car, the text of each walk does contain a grid reference giving the exact parking location.

The Country Code

The Country Code, as follows, makes sound common sense and should be observed at all times:

Enjoy the countryside and respect its life and work
Guard against all risk of fire
Fasten all gates
Keep your dogs under close control
Keep to public paths across farmland
Use gates and stiles to cross fences, hedges and walls
Leave livestock, crops and machinery alone
Take your litter home
Help to keep all water clean
Protect wildlife, plants and trees
Take special care on country roads
Make no unnecessary noise

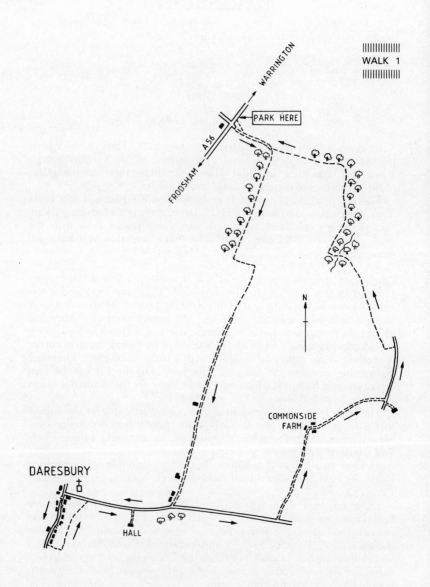

WALK 1

WARRINGTON

PARK HERE

A56

FRODSHAM

N

COMMONSIDE
FARM

DARESBURY

HALL

DARESBURY

★

4 miles (6.5 km)

OS Landranger 108

Visitors come from all over the world to Daresbury. The reason for their pilgrimage is that Lewis Carroll, the author of *'Alice's Adventures in Wonderland'*, was born here, and all over the village there are reminders of the colourful characters depicted in his stories.

The A56 road runs between Warrington and Frodsham. Three miles from Warrington, and opposite Hobb Lane, there is a roadside parking area close to a stile, and a footpath sign which points away from the road. There is a field gate nearby, so make sure that you have left enough room for access to the field. (Map ref. 587 839).

On leaving the car, go over the stile and walk up a facing track. After 180 metres the track reaches level ground. There are trees and a low sunken pond on the right here. Turn right on passing the trees and walk along a field edge with the trees on your immediate right. After 300 metres the trees finish. Go over a facing stile and turn left to walk along a field edge, keeping a fence on the left. After 60 metres the field corner is reached. Turn right and continue with a hedge on the left. There are contrasting views to the left and right here. On the left can be seen typical rolling pastures, whilst over to the right are the industrial towns of Runcorn and Widnes.

The path leads to a facing field gate. Go over a stile at the side of this gate and enter a gravel track which passes between hedgerows. Shortly pass stables, which are topped by an attractive ornate clock, and continue past a farm. A facing macadam drive leads to a crossing road, close to a pair of bungalows. Turn right, and follow the roadside footpath. Pass Daresbury Hall, and descend, to arrive at Daresbury Parish Church.

There has been a church at Daresbury since 1159, but the present building dates from 1872, with the exception of the tower, which was constructed during the 16th century. The church contains the famous 'Lewis Carroll Window', which was constructed in 1934, and shows scenes from *Alice's Adventures in Wonderland*. Various booklets and post-cards are on sale, and a glance through the visitors book shows that people have visited this place from the far corners of the globe. The church contains rich woodwork, and there is a ring of 8 bells, 4 of which date from 1725.

On leaving the church, turn right to enter the village. Straight ahead is the Ring O'Bells Inn and at its left hand side are the Parish Hall and the Lewis Carroll Centre. The latter is in the former Sessions House which, together with an adjoining barn have been restored to provide an exhibition and study centre. Turn left and walk into the main body of the village. Pass a mixture of cottages and other dwellings and continue past the school, on the roof of which can be seen an amusing weather vane, showing Alice chasing the Mad Hatter.

On passing the last dwelling in the village, enter a field on the left and walk forward keeping a hedge on your immediate left. Cross a stile at the field corner and turn left, to continue with a hedge on the left. After 90 metres go over a facing stile and cross a field, bearing diagonally right, to arrive at a stile near the field corner which is about 80 metres to the right of the church.

Turn right and walk back along the road by which you first arrived. Keep forward past the joining drive on the left, and walk forward along the road. After ½ mile arrive at the entrance drive of Commonside Farm, which is on the left. Leave the road here and walk along the drive in the direction of the farm. Go through the farmyard, turning right to pass between the farmhouse and outbuildings, then forward onto a facing track. A stile shortly takes you onto a crossing lane, where the way is left. (To the right, ¼ mile away, is Hatton village, and the Hatton Arms Inn).

Follow the lane for 200 metres to where, on the left, there is a stile and footpath sign. Go over the stile and enter a field. There is a hedge 30 metres away. Go over a stile which is set in a fence at the left hand side of the hedge. Continue with the hedge on your right at first, then bearing gradually left, go over a stile in a crossing hedge to enter a long rough field. Walk forward keeping near the left hand edge of the field and after 350 metres go over a stile which leads into a wood. The path runs over a crossing dyke via an earth and stone bank. About 30 metres farther on, the path traverses a stream via a large plank. Keep forward now along a well-worn path which climbs through trees and under-growth. Emerge from the trees over a stile and enter a large field. Turn right and proceed with trees on your immediate right. After 250 metres the path gradually turns to the left, and climbs along the field edge. There are still trees on the immediate right. The trees on the right finish shortly, but keep forward now and follow a track across the facing field, to arrive at the right hand side of a group of trees.

You are now back on part of the original route. Walk forward and descend along a facing track, to arrive back at the car, which is parked straight ahead.

CROWTON

WALK 2

★

4¾ miles (7.5 km)

OS Landranger 117

This pleasant walk passes through a very pretty area of Cheshire, where country lanes, field paths, hedged-in tracks and a stroll alongside the river Weaver combine to make an interesting excursion.

The B5153 road runs between Kingsley and Crowton. Half a mile to the west of Crowton village centre, a lane called Crewood Common leaves the B5153 road in a northerly direction. Drive along Crewood Common for just over ½ mile and park the car on the left, where there is good verge parking. (Map ref. 572 755).

On leaving the car, walk forward and pass Ainsworth Lane, which is on the right. Keep forward past lanes on left and right. There are cottages on the left now. The lane descends. Pass 2 rows of tiny cottages which are on the right. The lane leads to a robust footbridge which crosses a tributary of the river Weaver. Cross the bridge, then keep forward along a narrow macadam path. After 100 metres arrive at the river Weaver. Turn right and go through a gate to follow a path which keeps along the riverbank. Pass under the huge, 20-arch structure of Dutton Railway Viaduct. Negotiate a stile, and continue along the riverside. A further stile takes you to the side of a large lock.

Leave the river to the right now, where a stile in a crossing hedgerow leads into a field. Walk forward, keeping a hedgerow on your immediate left, and go over a stile at the field corner. Turn right and go over a stile at the side of a field gate then climb along a facing track. At the top of the climb go over 2 stiles in quick succession and walk forward to enter a facing lane. There is a farm on the right here. Pass dwellings on the right, then follow the lane as it bends to the left. Follow the lane past dwellings on left and right. Arrive at a junction of lanes and turn left. After ¼ mile, walk past Pear Tree Lane, which is on the right. About 50 metres further on, turn right and enter Chapel Lane. Acton Methodist Church is at the head of this lane. Follow Chapel Lane past Orchard Avenue to where, after ¼ mile, it passes over the railway. The lane turns sharply to the right here, but keep forward and enter a bridleway. Follow this hedged-in track for ½ mile, to where it descends and emerges from the hedges, close to a crossing stream. Go over a small bridge here, and pass through a facing gate which leads into a field. Climb forward along the field edge, keeping a hedge on your immediate right. Go through a second gate at the field corner, and

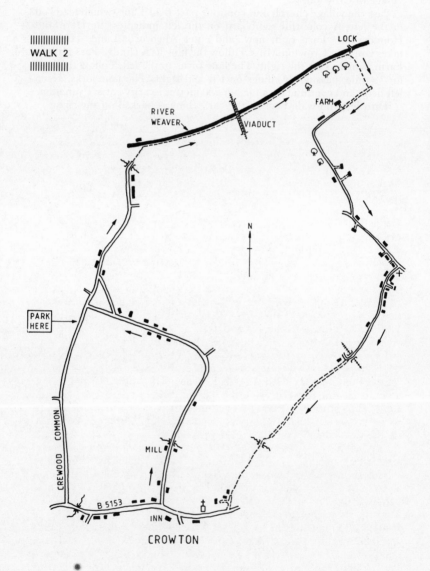

LOCK

RIVER
WEAVER

VIADUCT

FARM

N

PARK
HERE

CREWOOD COMMON

MILL

B 5153

INN

CROWTON

continue, once again keeping a hedge on your right. After 200 metres go through a facing gate. There are dwellings on the right here. Enter a track which leads onto a crossing road. Turn right and walk into the village of Crowton.

Pass the village church and continue past Bent Lane, which leads off to the left. A colourful signboard on the left indicates the Hare and Hounds Inn. Turn right now, and enter Ainsworth Lane. The lane takes you past Crowton Mills. Follow the lane as it climbs. Pass Hilltop Farm, which is on the right. The lane turns to the left. Follow the lane for ½ mile, passing dwellings on left and right. The lane forks. Keep left here, and continue for a further 250 metres to arrive at a T junction.

Turn left and walk back to the car, which is parked on the right.

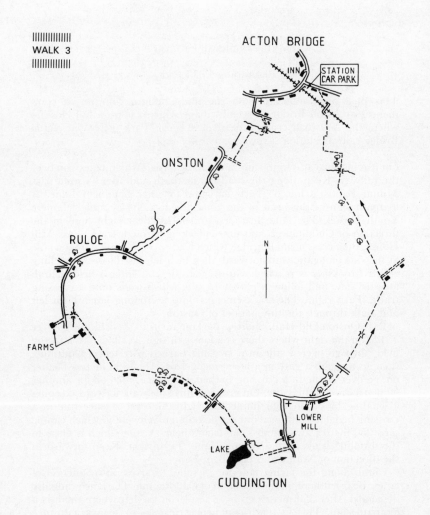

ACTON BRIDGE

INN

STATION CAR PARK

WALK 3

ONSTON

RULOE

FARMS

N

LOWER MILL

LAKE

CUDDINGTON

CUDDINGTON

WALK 3

★

5 miles (8 km)

OS Landranger 117 and 118

This pleasant ramble through the mid-Cheshire countryside commences at Acton Bridge, a scenic village which sits on a hill close to where the A49 road crosses the river Weaver. Park the car at Acton Bridge railway station. (Map ref. 599 747).

On leaving the car, climb steps and follow a road which takes you over the railway. Keep along the roadside footpath and after ¼ mile pass Milton Baptist Church. Turn left now to enter Sandfield Lane. A footpath sign at the head of the lane indicates Norley and Delamere Youth Hostel. The lane turns left and forks. Bear right here in the direction of Cuddington, and descend along a rough track. Pass Mill House, then cross a small bridge which leads over a brook. Cross a stile at the side of a gate, walk forward, then bear left just before a dwelling called Brookside is reached. Go over a stile and enter a field. Climb forward now and follow a path to a stile which leads onto a crossing track. Turn right. The track emerges onto a crossing lane. Turn left and walk through the tiny hamlet of Onston.

Pass Onston Old Hall. Shortly, the lane turns to the left, but go over a stile on the right where there is a footpath sign. Walk across a facing field, then go over a stile in a crossing barbed wire fence. Continue, then go through a gate in a facing hedgerow. About 90 metres farther on, go over a stile in a crossing barbed wire fence, then on for another 90 metres to another stile. On crossing this stile walk forward, keeping a winding brook on your immediate right. Go over a fence-stile in a crossing hedgerow and walk in the direction of a dwelling which can be seen 250 metres away across the facing field. A stile which is close to the dwelling leads onto a crossing lane. Turn right. Keep forward in the direction of Norley and pass Bent Lane.

Climb along the facing lane for ¼ mile, to arrive at a junction of lanes. Bear left here, in the direction of Cuddington. The lane gradually descends. After 350 metres go over a stile on the left where there is a footpath sign. This footpath commences just before a farm entrance drive on the right is reached. Walk across a level field for 60 metres, then cross an earth-topped bridge which leads over a brook. Bear slightly right now and climb, keeping a row of telegraph poles on your left. Go over a stile in a crossing fence. Pass close to farm outbuildings and climb along a facing track keeping a hedge and an old stone wall

17

on your right. On reaching the top of the hill bear left and continue along a field edge, keeping a hedge and fence on your immediate right. This section of path presents a fine vantage point for far-reaching views across the rolling countryside.

Go over a substantial wooden stile at the field corner and descend. Bear right at the bottom of the hill and arrive at 2 facing stiles. Go over the stile on the left and climb along a field edge, keeping a fence and trees on your immediate right. On reaching more level ground follow the path along the field edge and pass over 2 further stiles, then continue along a hedged-in track. The track emerges onto a crossing lane. Turn left, then almost immediately right, to follow a concrete drive which takes you past a small cottage. After 60 metres enter a fenced-in path which descends towards a lake. Cross a footbridge, then follow a narrow path which takes you past the lake. Bear left at a junction of paths and go over a stile which leads onto a track. Walk forward and emerge onto a crossing lane. Turn left, pass dwellings, and walk up the lane, which rises to arrive, after 400 metres, at a junction of lanes. Turn right here and walk past the Methodist Church, Cuddington. Descend, and at the bottom of the hill walk past the entrance drive of Lower Mill.

The lane leads over a bridge. About 80 metres farther on turn left, and leave the lane to pass through a kissing gate which is opposite some houses. Follow a path through trees, where there is a stream down on the left. The path runs past a bramble covered hillside on the right, then climbs up a facing bank. Go over a crossing road via 2 stiles and keep forward across a large field. After 250 metres go over a plank-bridge and a stile in a crossing hedge. A dwelling can be seen across the next field. The path leads across the field in the direction of the dwelling. Arrive close to the dwelling, then turn left and cross 2 fence-stiles in quick succession. Turn left and walk past the head of a drive which obviously connects the dwelling with the outside world. Walk along the edge of a large field, keeping a hedgerow on your immediate right. After 300 metres go over a stile which is set in a short crossing hedge.

Continue along the left-hand edge of 3 further fields, passing over stiles en route. A stile at the side of a gate leads out of the third field. Bear diagonally right now and walk under power cables. The path takes you to a crossing brook. Go over the brook via a small footbridge and a couple of stiles. Climb forward away from the footbridge keeping a hedge of trees and a fence on your immediate left. At the top of the hill turn left and proceed, still keeping a hedge and fence on your left. Turn right at the field corner and follow the fieldside hedgerow to a stile at the corner of the field. Cross the stile, turn right, then cross a second stile and turn left, to proceed with a hedgerow on your immediate left. Pass under telephone wires, then go over a stile at the field corner. The path leads to a large footbridge which crosses the railway. Go over this bridge, then follow a narrow fenced-in path which takes you past the rear of some dwellings. Arrive at a crossing road.

Turn left and walk back to Acton Bridge railway station and the car.

SHOTWICK

★

4¾ miles (7.5 km)

OS Landranger 117

For many centuries the village of Shotwick was an important point for travellers journeying to Wales and beyond. A ford and ferry lay close to the village, and these were in constant use prior to the silting of the Dee Estuary. Today the village lies at the end of a narrow lane, only ½ mile from a busy main road, but nevertheless one still feels miles away from the hurly-burly of modern life when passing through it.

The Yacht Inn sits by the side of the A540 road, midway between Chester and Neston. Leave the car on a roadside parking area which is by the A540 road, close to the inn. (Map ref. 354 732).

On leaving the car, walk towards the inn, then turn right just before the inn is reached, to proceed along a narrow lane. Follow this lane for 1 mile, to arrive at a crossing road. Take care here as the road is usually quite busy. Enter a facing lane where a sign says, 'Shotwick Village Only'. Walk along this lane, and in ½ mile, arrive at the tiny pictures-que village of Shotwick. The way is right now to enter a lane which commences opposite Stone Cottage, but first of all wander forward and have a look at the delightful village church.

Enter the lane opposite Stone Cottage, and keep forward past a turn-off to the left. Shortly, Shotwick Hall Farm is reached, which is on the right. You are now walking along part of the old 'Saltesway', an ancient highway which ran between the village and Shotwick Castle, which, alas, has long since disappeared. Turn left shortly and enter a rough track between hedgerows where a footpath sign indicates Puddington. Go through a gate which leads into a field. Keep forward, with a fence and hedge on your left. After 150 metres turn right at a crossing hedge. Continue for 20 metres, then turn left to pass through a pair of small gates. Turn right and continue with a fence and hedge now on your right. After 200 metres turn left, pass under power cables, and walk close to a pond which is on the right. On passing the pond, bear diagonally right and walk forward to shortly enter a large field. There is a large dwelling and garden over to the right here. The footpath, now diagonally right across the field, takes you to a gate which gives access to a drive. Turn left and follow the drive through an avenue of trees. Pass a farm entrance drive on the left, then dwellings on the right. Keep forward at a junction of ways and continue along a facing lane, to emerge at a bend in a crossing road. Turn right, and proceed along the

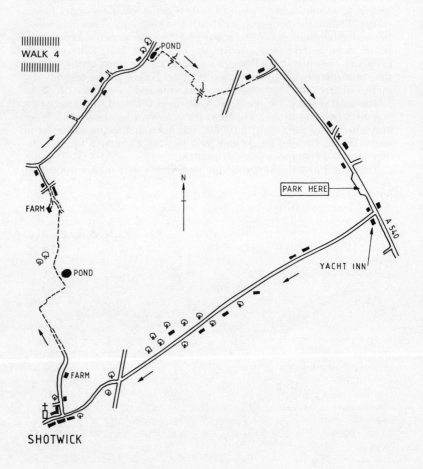

WALK 4

POND

N

FARM

POND

PARK HERE

A 540

YACHT INN

FARM

SHOTWICK

road for ½ mile, to where it bends right, and left, close to a dwelling called 'Windfalls'. There is a stile on the right, where the road straightens out, and a footpath sign which reads 'Two Mills'.

Cross the stile and enter a large field. Keep forward for a short distance, then turn left to skirt around a small pond. Turn right at a crossing hedge and continue, keeping the hedge on your immediate left. Cross a dyke at the field corner via a stile and a small wooden plank-bridge. Continue, again keeping a hedge on the left. Pass under power cables. Follow the hedgerow as it turns to the right. Turn left where the hedgerow finishes. Walk forward in the same general direction as before, with a dyke and a fence on your left at first, followed by a hedgerow once again. Go through a gate on the left, pass over a stream, then immediately go through a second gate. Follow a field edge for 200 metres to arrive at a crossing road via a stile and gate. Take care here as the road is usually quite busy. Walk over the road, then go over a stile in a crossing hedge. The footpath is hemmed-in between a fence and a hedgerow for a short distance, and leads to a facing stile close to outbuildings. Cross the stile and walk forward to enter a facing lane. The lane takes you to a crossing road.

Turn right and follow a roadside path for ½ mile, to arrive back at the car.

WHITEGATE

WALK 5

★

5¾ miles (9 km)

OS Landranger 118

Between the river Weaver and the tiny picturesque village of Whitegate is an area of unspoilt parkland. This is Vale Royal Park, once the setting of one of the finest abbeys in England. Sadly this once magnificent building has long since disappeared, being replaced by a large private house, but nevertheless we are fortunate that a public footpath still runs through this scenic area of countryside.

The A556 road crosses the river Weaver at Hartford Bridge. On the Chester side of the river there is a narrow lane which leads away from the A556 road. This lane is headed by a footpath sign. Park the car at the head of this lane where there is a gravel parking area. There are gates close by, so please leave enough room for access. (Map ref. 646 713).

On leaving the car, enter the narrow lane. This tree-lined lane runs parallel to the river and takes you under a railway viaduct. Quarter of a mile further on ascend some old stone steps on the right and climb for a short distance through rhododendron bushes, then go over a stile, which leads into a very large field. Bear diagonally left and follow a well-worn path across the field. The path leads to a wood. Cross a stile and descend steps to enter the wood. The way is forward through the trees. The path leads over a crossing path then traverses a stream. The path takes you to a stile in a crossing fence. Go over the stile and walk forward across a large field in the direction of trees which can be seen ¼ mile away, straight ahead.

Over to the left can be seen the private dwelling of Vale Royal, a large house, which sits on the old foundations of St Mary's Abbey.

Turn right just before the trees and follow the field edge, keeping a fence on your immediate left. After almost ½ mile emerge onto a crossing lane. Turn left, pass The Vicarage, and descend into the village of Whitegate.

On the right stands the church. There has been a church on this site since medieval times, but the present building dates from 1875. Further on from the church is the village green, where maypole dancing still takes place. Turn left now by a delightful thatched cottage, and enter Grange Lane. Pass dwellings then bear left and climb along Mill Lane. Pass Sutton Field on the left, and follow Mill Lane as it bears to the right. Pass the entrance drive of Bark House Farm and follow the lane

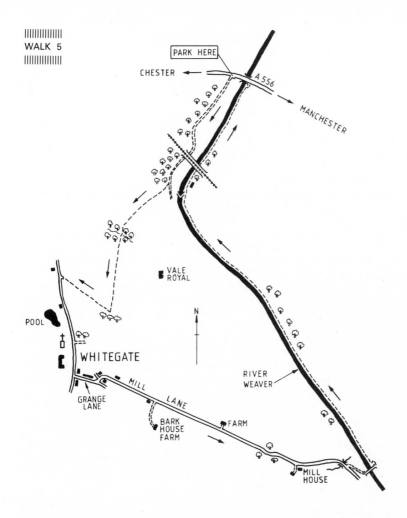

WALK 5

for a further mile, passing a farm on the left, and Mill House, an old restored water mill on the right. The lane turns to the right, and leads over a bridge. Cross the bridge, then leave Mill Lane to the left to follow a lane which leads to a pair of bridges which traverse the river Weaver. Cross the river, then turn left to follow a well-worn riverside path.

Follow the riverside for almost 2 miles; the path leads past Vale Royal Locks, then goes under a railway viaduct prior to reaching Hartford Bridge. Leave the riverside just before the bridge and climb to the right to reach the A556 road.

Turn left and cross the bridge to arrive back at the car, which is parked on the left.

23

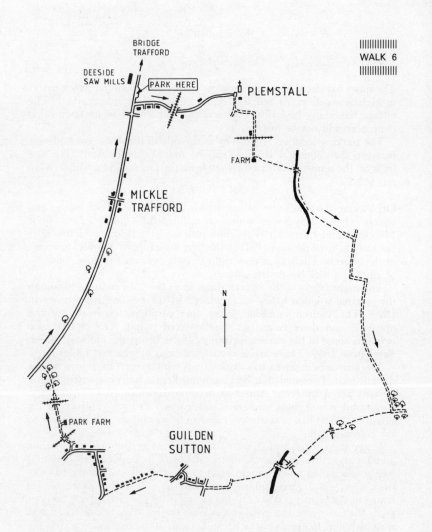

BRIDGE
TRAFFORD

DEESIDE
SAW MILLS

PARK HERE

PLEMSTALL

FARM

MICKLE
TRAFFORD

N

PARK FARM

GUILDEN
SUTTON

PLEMSTALL

WALK 6

★

5½ miles (9 km)

OS Landranger 117

The quiet hamlet of Plemstall lies less than 1 mile from the A56 Chester to Helsby road, yet it remains remote and largely undisturbed. The village has many historical connections, and a visit to its fascinating church should not be missed.

The parking location is a lay-by at the side of the A56 road mid-way between the villages of Bridge Trafford and Mickle Trafford. The lay-by is on the opposite side of the road from the Deeside Saw Mills. (Map ref. 449 703).

On leaving the car, enter a lane which begins close to the lay-by and which is headed by a sign which says, 'Plemstall Church'. Pass Glebe Meadows and Plemstall Way, then pass under a bridge which carries the railway over the lane. Follow the lane for a further ½ mile, to arrive at the church. The way is now right to pass over a cattle grid, but first of all take a look inside the church.

The main fabric of the church dates from the 15th century, although the original wooden belfry was replaced by the existing stone tower in 1825. The church contains many fine carvings, especially of the apostles, and there is an old double-tiered pulpit. The church also contains some of the earliest printings of the Bible, the oldest of which dates from 1549. There are also early editions of 'chained bibles'.

The surrounding area has associations which reach back into the far distant past. It is said that St Plegmund kept a hermitage here before he was asked by King Alfred to become Archbishop of Canterbury. Plegmund was a most energetic and learned Primate, and up to his death in AD 914 he was always eager to bring culture and literature to the common folk.

Leave the church and go over the cattle grid as directed, to continue along a gravel track. After 50 metres the track forks. Keep left here and follow a winding track which leads to the railway. Cross the railway lines here, via 2 gates, taking great care to ensure that there are no trains in the vicinity. Walk down a facing track towards a farm. Do not enter the farmyard, but go over a stile on the left. Pass a large barn and walk to a flat footbridge which can be seen 70 metres away across the facing field. The footbridge traverses the river Gowy. Cross the foot-bridge and turn right. Walk along the river bank and pass over a stile. The path leads over a dyke close to the river. Bear left here, and walk away from the river, aiming to the left of a large detached house which can be seen sitting on the highest ground straight ahead. After 200 metres the path crosses a dyke, then leads into a hedged-in track. Continue for 70 metres, then go over a stile at the side of a facing gate. There is a junction of paths here. Turn right and follow another hedged-in track.

Keep forward and follow the track as it turns left, then right. Proceed along the track for a further ½ mile, to where it turns sharply to the left in trees. Go over a stile on the right here, which is set between 2 gates. Descend along a field edge keeping a hedge on your immediate left. Go over a stile in a crossing fence. Keep forward for 100 metres, then cross a stile on the left. Turn right and continue with a hedge now on the right. Cross a small footbridge, followed by a stile, and enter a large field. Bear diagonally left and walk towards a gateway which can be seen to the right of a group of trees, 300 metres away. Go through the gateway and immediately cross a flat concrete bridge which takes you over a dyke. Turn right and quickly cross a second similar bridge which traverses the river Gowy. Immediately on crossing this second bridge go over a stile on the left. Turn right, then almost immediately left to follow a field edge, keeping a hedge on the immediate right. Follow the hedge as it bends to the right. After 350 metres cross a stile which is at the side of a field gate. Turn left, then follow a hedged-in track as it turns to the right.

Continue along the track, go over a stile, cross a road and enter Cinder Lane. Keep forward, pass Cinder Close, then enter a tree-lined track on the right. Descend through trees and emerge onto a crossing road. Turn left and pass the Bird In Hand Inn. Enter a tree-lined macadam lane. After 40 metres turn right through a kissing gate. Climb through trees and pass through a second kissing gate. Follow a facing macadam path which runs at the rear of new property. Keep forward along this path for over ¼ mile, to emerge at a bend in a crossing lane. Turn right. A straight stretch of lane takes you past dwellings and leads to a T-junction. Turn left here in the direction of Pipers Ash. After 250 metres the road bends to the left, but go right here to enter a track which commences close to a house called Firwood. Bear left and follow the track over the railway.

Keep forward past Park Farm. Pass under a bridge which carries the railway over the footpath. Go over a facing stile and continue along a hedged-in path. The path takes you to a crossing road via a stile. Go over the road and turn right to follow the roadside pavement.

Keep forward for 1 mile, passing through the centre of Mickle Trafford village en route, to arrive back at the car.

26

TARVIN

WALK 7

★

6½ miles (10.5 km)

OS Landranger 117

Four villages, Ashton, Tarvin, Oscroft and Kelsall, are visited during the course of this walk, which passes through some typical Cheshire scenery.

The B5393 road joins the A54 road mid-way between Kelsall and Tarvin. One mile to the north of this junction is the village of Ashton. On the northern side of the village, and by the side of the B5393 road, there is a long roadside verge at the bottom of a hill between Mouldsworth railway station and Ashton church. This parking area is between Delamere Road and Grange Road. (Map ref. 511 703).

On leaving the car, walk along the road in the direction of Ashton church and pass Grange Road. Continue past the church and at the junction of roads ahead keep forward in the direction of Tarvin. Turn right on reaching the Golden Lion Inn and enter West End, a lane which winds between attractive old cottages. On passing West End Cottage the lane turns left and takes you to cross-roads. Keep forward here and enter Whitegate Lane. The lane leads into a hedged-in track. Follow this track for 400 metres to where there is a sign on the left which says, 'Public Footpath—Tarvin Sands'. Go over the stile here and walk straight across a facing field. Pass over a stile in a crossing hedge then bear slightly right to cross the next field. Pass through a gate in a crossing hedge and keep forward with a hedge on the immediate left. On reaching the field corner go straight over a farm approach drive.

Continue, keeping a hedge on your immediate right. After 150 metres the hedge turns to the left, but keep forward over a stile to enter a large field. Keep forward in the same general direction as before and walk over a small wooden plank-bridge which takes you over Salters Brook. Proceed past an isolated tree and cross a large field keeping a hedge on the left about 60 metres away. On meeting a crossing hedge go over a stile and continue with a hedge on the left. After 150 metres go over a stile at the side of a gate and pass straight over a crossing lane to enter a facing lane. The lane emerges onto the A54 road. Cross the road, and take care as this road is usually quite busy. Turn right, then almost immediately left to follow a road which leads away from the A54 road. Pass cottages, some of which are set on foundations of solid sandstone rock. Arrive at a junction of roads in the centre of Tarvin village.

The village contains many beautiful Georgian buildings constructed

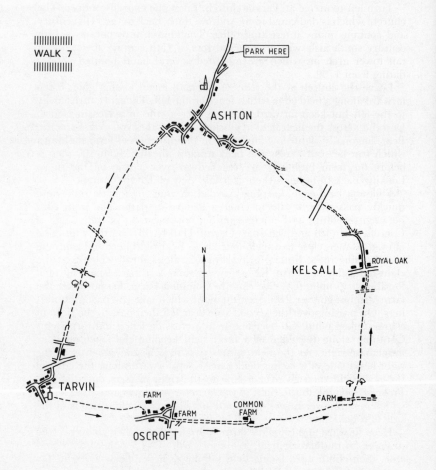

||||||||||||||
WALK 7
||||||||||||||

PARK HERE

ASHTON

N

KELSALL   ROYAL OAK

TARVIN

FARM

FARM

COMMON
FARM

FARM

OSCROFT

28

in the wake of a disastrous fire in 1752 which destroyed many of the former timber-framed cottages. The village is famous for being the home of the 18th century penman, John Thomasen, who was also the local schoolmaster. Queen Anne was so impressed with his work that she commissioned him to transcribe the old Greek poets.

Turn left to arrive at Tarvin church. Enter the church confines. The church, which is dedicated to St Andrew, dates back to the 14th century and contains many interesting relics. The church incorporates a 14th century south aisle with its original roof, a 15th century tower and a tall tower arch on which are mounted several hand painted shields dating from 1700.

Leave the church at the rear, via a small metal kissing gate. Keep forward along a field edge with a fence on the left. The fence turns away to the left but keep forward, then go over a stile in a crossing fence. Descend across the next field to a bridge which takes you over a stream. Bear diagonally right now and walk in the direction of farm buildings which can be seen across the field straight ahead. About 100 metres before the farm buildings are reached go over a stile on the right. Looking back from here, there is a fine view of Tarvin church.

Follow a field edge, keeping a hedge on your immediate right, and quickly pass over a stile to enter a hedged-in path. The path runs between dwellings and emerges onto a crossing road in the village of Oscroft. Turn left and walk past Oscroft Hall Farm. Shortly, a junction of roads is met, close to a telephone kiosk. Bear right here and continue to a crossing road. Enter a gravel track straight ahead which is at the right-hand side of a farm. Keep forward along a straight length of track for almost ½ mile, to arrive close to Common Farm. Do not enter the farmyard but go over 2 stiles on the right which take you past outbuildings. On passing over the second stile bear left then pass to the right of a low sunken pond. Go over a stile in a crossing fence and turn right. Continue along the edge of a large field keeping the fence on your immediate right. At the field corner pass over a stile which is at the right-hand side of a facing field gate. Keep forward along the edge of the next field then go over a stile to the right of farm outbuildings. Proceed, keeping to the right of the farm outbuildings and cross a stile which is set between trees. Turn left and go over a stile which is at the side of a field gate.

Keep forward and cross the farm approach tracks then go over a stile to enter an undulating field. Walk forward, cross a plank-bridge and stile, then climb up a facing field keeping a hedge on your right. Go over a stile in a crossing fence. Keep forward in the same direction as before and cross 2 fields via stiles. Go over a crossing track and enter a narrow hedged-in path which commences through a metal gate at the right-hand side of a small wooden bungalow. The path emerges onto the A54 road opposite the Royal Oak Hotel in the village of Kelsall. Enter Frodsham Street, which commences at the left side of the hotel. The lane passes cottages and after 500 metres turns sharply to the left. Enter a hedged-in track on the right here where a sign says, 'Public

Footpath—Ashton'. This track commences close to the entrance of Northwood Hall Caravan Park. The track leads to a stile and steps which take you to the Kelsall by-pass. The way is straight across the by-pass—but be extremely careful here as the traffic is usually moving deceptively quickly. On crossing the by-pass descend steps and go over a stile.

Straight ahead, the spire of Ashton church comes into view. Aiming to the left of the church spire, follow a path which takes you along the left-hand edge of 4 fields and over 4 stiles. On crossing the 4th stile enter a hedged-in track and turn left. The track emerges onto a lane in the suburbs of the village of Ashton. Walk forward, passing Willowhayes, Pentre Close and Dunn's Lane to arrive at a road junction. Turn right. Pass Foxhunter Close which is on the left, and arrive at a T-junction. Turn right here in the direction of Frodsham.

You are now back on part of the original route. Walk past the church and back to the car, which is parked on the right.

CHESTER—CITY WALLS

WALK 8

★

2 miles (3 km)

OS Landranger 117

The ancient city walls of Chester are well known. These ramparts, the origins of which date back to Roman times, completely encircle the inner city, and to walk along them is to capture the very feeling of Chester's history.

The walk is unique because Chester is the only place in England where a complete circuit of ancient walls has been retained. Once access to the walls has been found it is impossible to get lost. Access points are numerous, and parking facilities generous, thus enabling the walk to commence at any convenient point.

A suggested parking place for this walk is outside the walls on the east side of Chester Cathedral, where a new, rather Germanic looking bell-tower stands alone at the south-east corner of the cathedral precincts overlooking a car park which lies just off Frodsham Street. (There is a nominal charge here.)

From the car park ascend a row of steps which lead onto the walls. Turn right and pass close to the cathedral. During the course of this walk there are numerous places where you can leave the walls and take a closer look at a place of interest before continuing—Chester Cathedral is one of these places.

The cathedral and its environs are most interesting. Standing on the site of a Saxon church, the present building dates from the 11th century. Previously an abbey, it became the Cathedral of the See of Chester in 1541, and has remained so ever since. A detailed account of its long and varied history is available inside.

At the north-east corner of the walls is King Charles' Tower. A tablet set into this tower says, 'King Charles stood on this tower September 24th 1645 and saw his army defeated on Rowton Moor'.

The walls now swing to the west where they run high above the Shropshire Union Canal. As the Northgate is approached the Bluecoat Hospital can be seen over to the right. A close look reveals a Bluecoat Boy standing over the entrance door reading a book. The walls gradually descend from the Northgate, and lead past Morgans Mount, a small watch-tower from which there is a fine view. If the day is clear the Welsh hills can be seen straight ahead. The walls traverse the new ring-road and lead to the Goblin Tower. Originally completely round

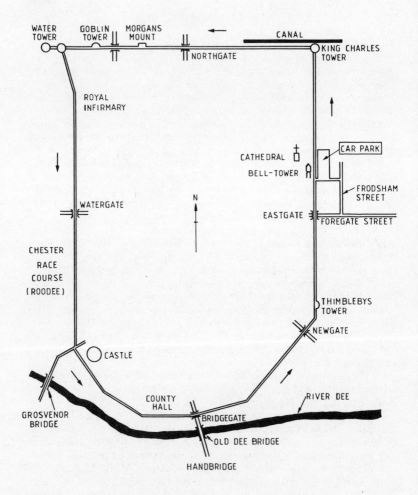

when first erected during the 13th century, more recent renovations have left this tower a rather odd semi-circular shape.

At the north-west corner of the walls stands Bonewaldesthorne Tower. This tower stands close to where the river once flowed, and as the waters gradually receded due to silting, a second tower was built at a lower level. This second tower is called the Water Tower, and the 2 towers are connected by a flight of steps. At the base of these towers, and outside the walls, there is an attractive parkland setting.

The walls now head southwards and descend to road level. Keep forward and pass in front of the Royal Infirmary, which dates from 1761. Pass the fine old Georgian houses of Stanley Place and then climb over Watergate to continue where the walls run parallel with Nun's Road. Over to the right is the Roodee, where horse racing has been held since 1512. The remains of an old cross can still be seen protruding from the meadow.

The route now crosses Grosvenor Road and runs parallel with Castle Drive. On the left is Chester Castle. A Saxon stronghold once stood on this site, but the present castle contains a contrasting mixture of medieval and 19th century buildings. The large stone arch of Grosvenor Bridge comes into view over to the right. This fine structure carries the road to Wales over the river Dee.

Shortly after passing County Hall ascend Bridgegate. There are charming views from here. On the city side can be seen the Bear and Billet Inn, which dates from 1664. The inn, which has richly carved gables, faces a row of delightful Georgian houses. On the river side of Bridgegate is the 'old' Dee Bridge which connects the city with Handbridge. This fine medieval stone bridge has seen generations of Handbridge fishermen net the famous Dee salmon as they negotiate the nearby weir which leads them to higher waters.

The walls shortly climb away from the river and turn in a northerly direction. Shortly after passing a renovated Roman hypocaust arrive at Newgate, which takes the walls over Little St John Street. One of the largest Roman amphitheatres yet discovered has been excavated just outside the walls here.

The walls now wind past more modern buildings and lead past the remains of Thimbleby's Tower to Eastgate, where a narrow bridge, topped by an ornate Victorian clock, passes over Chester's main shopping street. This street contains the famous Rows—2 tiers of shops where the top tier is protected by an overhang which forms a protective balcony. A few more metres and you have completed one of the finest walks in any English city.

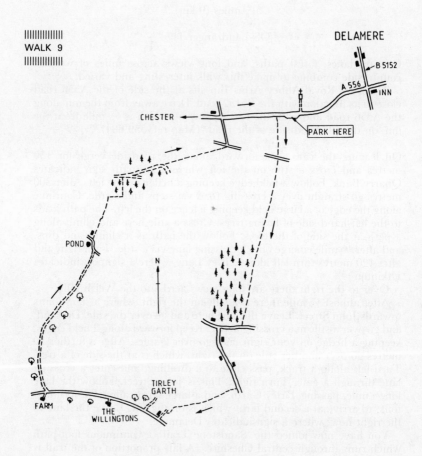

TIRLEY

WALK 9

★

5½ miles (9 km)

OS Landranger 117

Country lanes, forest paths, and long views across miles of wooded countryside combine to make this walk interesting and varied.

The Vale Royal Abbey Arms Inn sits at the side of the A556 road close to its junction with the B5152 road. Drive away from the inn along the A556 road and park the car in a lay-by which is ⅓ mile from the inn, on the left-hand side of the road. (Map ref. 559 684).

On leaving the car, walk forward along the roadside verge for 150 metres and cross a stile on the left where a footpath sign indicates Quarry Bank. Follow a field edge keeping a hedge on the left. After 300 metres go straight over a crossing road via steps and a stile. Continue along the edge of a large field keeping a fence on the left. The path leads to the left-hand side of facing trees. Cross a stile here and climb along a path at the side of the trees. Follow the path as it climbs and dips, and after ½ mile emerge onto a crossing lane via a stile. Turn right and after 120 metres turn left along Tirley Lane, where a signpost indicates Utkinton.

Over to the right there are long views across to the Welsh hills.

After almost ½ mile there is a stile on the right, where a sign points towards John Street. Leave the lane here and go over the stile. Descend, and go over a stile in a crossing hedge. Keep forward along 2 field edges, keeping a hedge on your right, and go over 2 stiles. After a further 20 metres go over another stile on the right, which is at the side of a tree. Turn left along a track, pass close to a dwelling, and enter a crossing lane through a gate. Turn right. This is John Street. Follow the lane for ½ mile, passing Tirley Garth, and a large farm called The Willingtons, to arrive at a second farm which is on the left. Leave the lane to the right now, where a sign indicates Delamere.

You have now joined the 'Sandstone Trail', a continuous foot-path which runs through central Cheshire. (A fair proportion of the trail is covered by a series of circular walks in Cheshire Walks for Motorists). Climb along a facing track where there are fine views shortly, over to the left. After ¾ mile emerge onto a crossing lane and turn left. After 50 metres go through a facing gateway where a sign indicates Delamere Forest. There is a dwelling on the left here. Enter a narrow hedged-in path over a stile. Cross another stile and continue along a field edge with a hedge on the right. Go through a kissing gate and proceed with a hedge now on the left. Descend, and go over a stile which leads into trees.

The Sandstone Trail turns to the left here, but turn right now, and leave the trail. After 50 metres turn left and follow a straight path between trees. After 120 metres walk straight over a crossing track and bear right to follow a track which descends between trees. After 300 metres the track turns sharply to the right. Leave the track here and go over a facing stile to enter a large field. Walk across the field in the same direction as the track you have just walked down—aiming towards a low-lying brick structure which can be seen across the field straight ahead. Go over a stile at the side of the brick structure and keep forward in the same general direction as before. Go over 2 further stiles to arrive at a crossing road. Enter a facing lane. After 200 metres another crossing road is met.

Turn right now and follow the roadside verge for ¼ mile, to arrive back at the car.

CHRISTLETON

WALK 10

★

5 miles (8 km)

OS Landranger 117

The majority of this particular walk is by way of quiet, country lanes, which meander through a very interesting portion of the Cheshire countryside.

Turn off the A51 Chester Road close to its junction with the B5132 road at Stamford Bridge, and drive down a lane which is headed by a sign which says, 'Cotton Edmunds'. Pass Green Lane, which is on the right, and park the car on the left, where there is good verge parking. (Map ref. 464 668).

Leave the car and proceed down the lane. The lane winds past farm and cottage. One mile after leaving the car, arrive at a T-junction where a minor lane joins from the left. Keep right here, and follow the lane as it turns to the right. Continue along the lane for a further ¾ mile, to arrive at crossroads, shortly after passing the Plough Inn. Turn left here along Brown Heath Road in the direction of Waverton and Whitchurch. A straight 600 metres leads to a track on the right where a footpath sign indicates Rowton Bridge. The footpath begins at the side of a house called 'Oaklands'. After 70 metres, cross a stile and enter a field. Walk forward, keeping a hedge on your right, then go over 2 stiles in quick succession. Continue, still keeping a hedge on your right, and go over another stile near the field corner. Climb through trees to arrive on the towpath of the Shropshire Union Canal. Turn right and walk along the canal towpath.

During 1645 the bloody Battle of Rowton Moor took place in the fields on the other side of the canal.

Cross 2 stiles then, on meeting a facing hedgerow, turn right and climb slightly to arrive at a stile. Cross the stile and follow a narrow, hedged-in passageway to emerge onto a facing lane. Keep forward along this lane which takes you past large detached houses. On meeting a T-junction turn right. Keep forward in the direction of the church tower which shortly comes into view, peeping over trees, straight ahead. You are now entering the village of Christleton. Proceed past the Ring O'Bells Inn and arrive at St James's Church, which is on the left.

A church has stood on this site since 1093, but the present building was constructed in 1877, with the exception of the tower, which dates from the 15th century. The church looks out across the village green at the side of which is The Pump and Pumphouse. Christleton has won

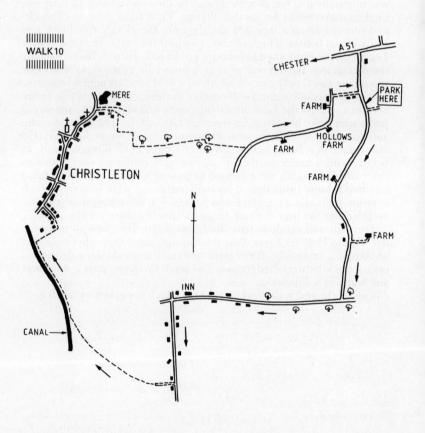

the coveted Best Kept Village award 3 times and on a peaceful summer day it is hard to imagine the havoc caused by the Battle of Rowton Moor, when the majority of the village houses were burnt down by the Royalists.

Leave the village green in the direction of Tarvin and Northwich and walk along Heath Road. Pass Christleton Methodist Church and arrive at a small mere which is on the right. Known locally as 'The Pit', it was originally dug out as a marl pit. The limy clay known as marl was used to make bricks for local buildings. Turn right prior to 'The Pit' and proceed along a lane. On the right are the picturesque black and white Dixon houses. The lane takes you past the entrance to the British Legion on the right, then to cottages on the left. Turn right on reaching the cottages on the left and go over a fence-stile at the right-hand side of a facing metal field gate. Walk along a field edge keeping a hedgerow on your immediate right. Go through a narrow gap in a crossing hedge and turn left. At the field corner turn right and arrive at a junction of paths where the hedgerow on your left turns to the left. Turn left here and continue, again keeping a hedgerow on your immediate left. Go over a stile in a facing hedge and enter a large field. Keep forward, as before, with a hedge on the left. At the field corner go over a stile to enter trees, then turn right and left to go over another stile which takes you into a large field. Bear diagonally right and walk to a stile which is to the right of a gate which can be seen 150 metres away in a hedge on the right. Go over the stile to join a crossing lane.

Turn left and continue past Birchbank Farm. The lane turns to the left close to Hollows Farm. Pass the entrance drive of another farm and walk past a bungalow. Turn right now and leave the lane to enter a grassy track between hedgerows. The track takes you past 2 dwellings and leads to a T-junction.

Turn right and walk back to the car, which is parked on the left.

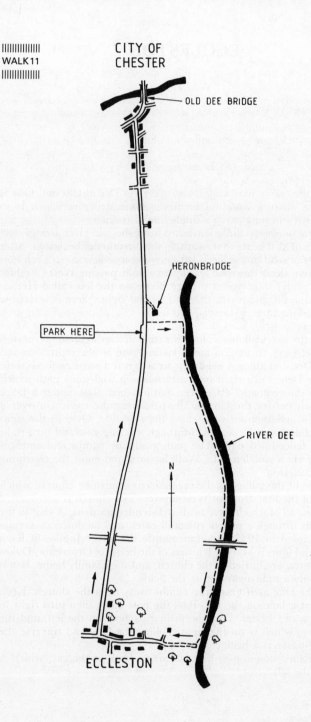

||||||||||||
WALK 11
||||||||||||

CITY OF
CHESTER

OLD DEE BRIDGE

HERONBRIDGE

PARK HERE

RIVER DEE

N

ECCLESTON

ECCLESTON

WALK 11

★

2¼ miles (3.5 km)

OS Landranger 117

Only 2 bridges carry road traffic over the river Dee at Chester. One is modern, the other a beautiful medieval stone structure which is so narrow that it can only carry a single line of traffic.

Drive in a southerly direction away from the 'old' Dee Bridge and follow the road as it bears to the right in the direction of Eccleston. After 140 metres the road forks. Keep left here where a sign says, 'Eccleston 2 miles'. Drive along this road for almost a mile, passing West Cheshire College en route, to arrive at a large house on the left called Heron-bridge. About 150 metres further on, on the right, there is a narrow roadside parking area. (Map ref. 410 639).

On leaving the car, walk back along the road in the direction of Chester. After 40 metres go through a metal kissing gate on the right, followed by a stile. Descend along a field edge to arrive at a crossing fence close to the river Dee. Turn right here and follow a well-worn path which runs along the riverside. Pass over 3 stiles then walk under a large bridge which carries the Chester By-pass over the river. Go over 2 further stiles and keep forward along the riverside. Over to the right Eccleston church can be seen. Go through a facing gate and turn right to follow a fence-lined path. The path gradually climbs and emerges onto a lane via a wooden gate. Walk forward and enter the charming village of Eccleston.

The pride of the village is the magnificent sandstone church, which was a gift of the first Duke of Westminster. The church is surrounded by dwellings, all of which have neat, well-tended gardens. A visit to the church leads through a pair of splendid gates, and on down an avenue of trees, planted in 1935 to commemorate the Silver Jubilee of King George V and Queen Mary. Members of the house of Grosvenor, Dukes of Westminster, are buried in the church, and their family home, Eaton Hall, lies only a mile away across the fields.

Follow the lane as it gradually climbs away from the church. Keep forward past a lane on the left. Pass the post office then turn right in the direction of Chester. Pass the primary school on the left, and the Old Rectory, which is on the right. Follow the lane and traverse the Chester By-pass via a bridge.

Keep forward now for ½ mile, to arrive back at the car, which is parked on the left.

HARGRAVE

WALK 12

★

4¾ miles (7.5 km)

OS Landranger 117

The village of Waverton lies 4 miles to the south-west of Chester, and ¼ mile to the east of the A41 road. Drive in a south-easterly direction away from the village centre, and continue along a road which goes towards Hargrave and then runs parallel to the Shropshire Union Canal. Arrive at a sharp left hand bend which takes the road over the canal via a narrow hump-backed bridge. Do not drive over this bridge, but park the car on the right, where there is verge parking available. There are field gates close by, so please leave enough room for access. (Map ref. 481 617).

On leaving the car, walk over the bridge. The lane forks. Keep forward here, in the direction of Hargrave. On the left shortly there is a private dwelling. When the survey for the original book was carried out in 1974, this dwelling was a tiny church. Keep forward past a lane on the left which goes to Waverton and Tarvin, to arrive at the church of St Peter, Hargrave.

Above the entrance there is a tablet informing us that 'Thomas Moulsone of Ye Citty of London, Alderman built this Chappell upon his owne cost and charge in 1627'. Moulsone was the son of a local farmer and eventually became Lord Mayor of London in 1634. The church is of plain sandstone construction and the hammer-beam roof is original. Unfortunately, most of the original fittings have been removed, but there is some interesting modern stained glass.

Enter a track at the left-hand side of the church then pass dwellings to go over a stile in a crossing hedge. Keep forward along a field edge and pass through a kissing gate which leads onto a lane. Turn right. After 100 metres follow the lane as it turns to the right. There is a no-through-road on the left here.

Follow this pleasant lane for almost 1½ miles, as it winds to left and right, passing a number of dwellings en route. Keep an eye open for a footpath sign on the left which says, 'Public Footpath—Waverton'. (Note—if you arrive at a T-junction you have journeyed 200 metres too far).

Go over a stile and walk straight across a facing field. On reaching a crossing hedge go over a stile at the side of a field gate. Continue, and pass to the right of a small pond. A further stile and footbridge take you onto a facing track where there is a wood on the right. Continue,

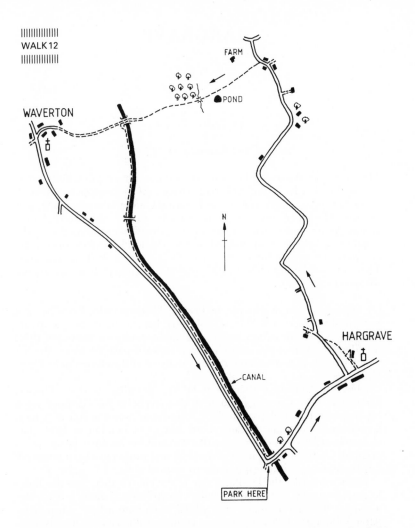

keeping a fence, ditch, and trees on your immediate right. At the field corner go over a tiny stile at the side of a gate and continue. Go over another stile and enter a hedged-in track. The track leads to a narrow hump-backed bridge which traverses the Shropshire Union Canal. Cross this bridge.

There are now 2 routes which you can follow:
1 There is a stile on the left which leads onto the canal tow-path. A gentle stroll of 1½ miles takes you back to where the car is parked.
2 The facing track leads to St Peter's Church. Follow the road past the church and shortly walk parallel to the canal and back to the car.

43

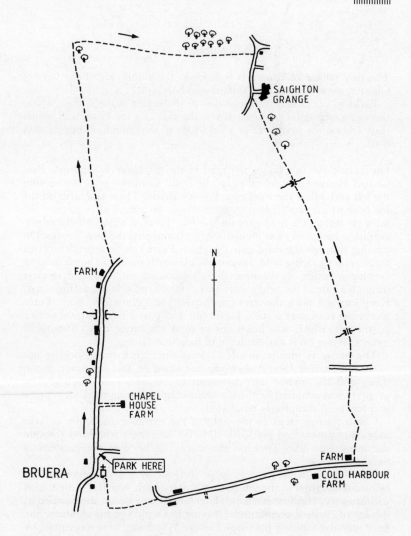

SAIGHTON
FARM

SAIGHTON
GRANGE

FARM

N

FARM

CHAPEL
HOUSE
FARM

BRUERA

PARK HERE

COLD HARBOUR
FARM

BRUERA

★

3½ miles (5.5 km)

OS Landranger 117

The tiny village of Bruera is 5 miles to the south-east of the City of Chester, midway between Aldford and Saighton.

Park the car close to a T-junction in the centre of the village, where there is a triangular parking area at the side of a low lying wall which runs around the perimeter of a field next to the church. (Map ref. 438 606).

On leaving the car, follow the road in the direction of Saighton. Pass Chapel House Farm which is on the right. Continue past cottages on the left and follow the road over Powsey Brook. There is a farm on the left here which was erected in 1891. About 80 metres after passing the farm go through a field gate on the left. Proceed along 3 field edges, keeping a hedge on your immediate right, and pass through 3 gates. On passing through the third gate, Saighton Farm can be seen 250 metres away across a facing field. Do not walk towards the farm, but turn right keeping a hedge on the immediate right, and walk forward to pass through a gate at the field corner at the right-hand side of a facing wood. Keep forward, with the trees on your left, and gradually climb. Enter a crossing road over a stile. Turn right and pass a farm entrance drive on the left, which was hewn out of solid sandstone rock. About 120 metres farther on is the entrance to Saighton Grange.

The house is ideally situated, being on high ground looking out towards the river Dee. A dwelling has stood on this site since Saxon times and the manor once belonged to the abbey at Chester. The property was acquired by the Grosvenor family during the 19th century and has been completely renovated.

Climb narrow steps to the right of the entrance and enter a large field. Go forward and gradually descend, keeping a fence and trees on the immediate left. Through the trees can be seen the gardens of Saighton Grange.

These magnificent gardens were laid out by Lady Grosvenor, the beautiful daughter of the 9th Earl of Scarborough. She had a life tinged with tragedy. Her first husband, Earl Grosvenor, whom she married at the age of 19, died prematurely, leaving her with 3 young children. She later married aspiring politician George Wyndham who was tipped by many as a future prime minister. However, Wyndham died before his political ambitions could be realised, and this, coupled with the death of her young son, brought about an illness from which she never recovered. These beautiful gardens therefore form a lasting tribute to the memory of a brave and tragic woman.

At the field corner, go over a concrete footbridge and continue along a field edge keeping a fence and a hedge on the immediate left. Pass over a stile in a crossing fence and continue along the edge of a large field, keeping a hedge on your immediate left. At the corner of the field pass over Powsey Brook via a small wooden footbridge. Keep forward across a narrow facing field then traverse a crossing lane via staggered stiles. Keep straight across a facing field and go over a stile in a crossing hedge. There is a small farmhouse straight ahead. Bear slightly left now and go over another stile. Keep forward with a hedge on the right and pass close to the farmhouse then enter a crossing lane over a stile. Turn right and follow the lane to shortly pass Cold Harbour Farm which is on the left.

Continue along the lane for a further ½ mile to where it turns sharply to the right, close to cottages. Leave the lane here over a facing stile to follow a field edge keeping a hedge and a brook on your immediate left. Traverse a shallow crossing ditch, then about 30 metres before reaching the end of the field, turn right and pass through a gap in a crossing hedgerow. Walk forward to shortly enter the confines of the church of St Mary the Virgin, Bruera, through a slatted field gate.

The church is only small but is sturdily built from sandstone rock. The chancel arch is Norman and the main fabric is said to contain Saxon stones. The small square turret is of shingle construction, being a strong wooden framework covered with wooden slates which contrasts with the large sandstone buttresses underneath it.

Leave the church via its lych gate and turn right to arrive back at the car, which is parked on the right.

CODDINGTON

★

8 miles (13 km)

OS Landranger 117

The scattered hamlet of Coddington lies amidst the lush green fields of the border country to the south of Chester. The walk, which commences close to the river Dee at Aldford, is easy going as it stays entirely on flat, level ground.

Driving south through Aldford on the B5130 road, pass the Grosvenor Arms Hotel then Rushmere Lane on the right, to turn down the next lane on the left, which is headed by a no-through-road sign. After 200 metres pass a track which goes off to the left and park the car on the left, where there is good verge parking available. (Map ref. 422 586).

On leaving the car, walk back along the lane you have just driven down. Turn right and pass the Grosvenor Arms Hotel. Follow the road as it passes over Aldford Brook via a stone bridge. The road turns left now but keep forward to enter a facing lane where road signs indicate a vehicle weight limit of 7.5T. Pass Chapel House and Grosvenor Cottage then turn right to enter a lane which is headed by a no-through-road sign.

Follow the lane, and after ½ mile pass dwellings on the left. The lane turns to the left near a large farm and then turns to the right close to farm outbuildings. Keep forward along the lane and pass over Aldford Brook once again. Pass Mill Cottage (1868). The lane becomes a stony track which shortly turns sharp right towards a farm. Do not follow the track as it turns to the right but enter a field through a facing gate and almost immediately turn left through a double gateway to enter a large field. Bear slightly right and walk forward to arrive at the right-hand side of a fenced-in pond where a solitary tree stands by the water. Continue across the field and walk in the direction of a gate which can be seen in a crossing hedgerow. This gate is about 160 metres to the right of a wood. On passing through the gate continue in the same direction as before and go through a gap in a crossing hedgerow. Proceed, and arrive at a gate which takes you onto a hedge-lined track. Turn right and after ¼ mile pass a duck-pond and farmhouse. Follow the facing farm approach drive for a further ½ mile, and emerge onto a crossing lane close to Middle Beachin Farm. Turn left and walk along the lane for 1 mile to arrive at the village of Coddington.

On the left is the 19th century church of St Mary. The area has many historical connections. General Massey, who was a friend and confidant

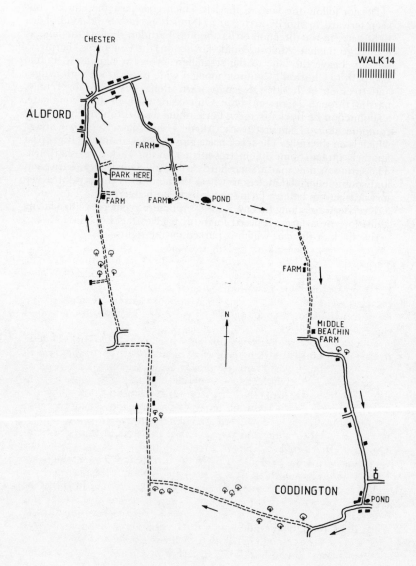

CHESTER

WALK 14

ALDFORD

FARM

PARK HERE

FARM

FARM

POND

FARM

N

MIDDLE
BEACHIN
FARM

CODDINGTON

POND

of Charles II lived close by. Indeed, it was Massey who rode with the defeated King after the Battle of Worcester in 1651, prior to his escape to France.

Do not follow the lane to the left which goes past the church, but keep forward to shortly arrive at a T-junction close by a pond. Turn right here, in the direction of Barton and Farndon. Follow the lane as it turns to the left. Almost ½ mile farther on, the lane turns sharply to the left. Leave the lane to the right here, where a sign says, 'Public Footpath to Churton'. Continue along a wide rough track with hedges and trees on both sides. Keep forward along this track for 1 mile, passing through 2 gates en route. On passing through the second gate, a T-junction of tracks is met. Turn right, pass through a gate, and continue along a narrow track. After ½ mile pass Royalty Cottage which is on the right. The track has a gravel surface now and leads past another cottage. Some 300 metres further on the track turns sharp left. The surface is now macadam. Shortly a crossing lane is met. Turn right and continue for 200 metres to where the lane turns sharp right. Keep forward here to enter a facing track between hedgerows.

Keep forward along this track for over a mile, to emerge onto a facing lane close by a farm. Proceed forward, pass cottages on the left, and arrive back at the car, which is parked on the right.

CLUTTON

WALK 15

FARNDON

PARK HERE

FARM

LODGE

HIGHER CARDEN

HALL

ISLE FARM

N

TILSTON

TILSTON

WALK 15

★

5½ miles (9 km)

OS Landranger 117

Almost the whole of this walk passes through the former estate of Carden, an estate which at one time filled the area between the villages of Clutton and Tilston.

The village of Clutton lies 3 miles to the east of Farndon on the A534 road. A lane leaves the village in a southerly direction. This lane is headed by a sign which ways, 'Carden ¾'. There is also another sign indicating an alternative route to Tilston. Park the car ⅓ mile down here on the right, close to where a footpath sign points towards Carden. (Map ref. 466 539). In the event of this parking area being full, there is verge parking available further up the lane on the left.

On leaving the car, go through a gate where the footpath sign points towards Carden. Follow the edge of a conifer wood and pass through a facing field gate. Continue, and where the wood finishes, look over to the right where there is a fine view across to the Welsh hills. There is a fence on the right now. Keep forward past a metal kissing gate. The path bends to the left and joins a gravel track where there is a low stone wall and trees on the right. Keep forward along the track then pass through a facing gate to enter a walled-in track. The track passes close to a farm and emerges onto a crossing lane. On the right here is the lodge gate entrance of Carden estates.

The estate once contained a magnificent timber hall but unfortunately this was burned down a number of years ago and there remains not a trace of its former splendour. Go forward, bearing left and follow the lane in the direction of Tilston. After almost ½ mile the lane takes you past the beautiful black and white Lower Carden Hall which is on the left. Keep forward for a further ½ mile, passing Isle Farm en route, to arrive at a crossroads in the centre of Tilston village.

There are 2 inns close by; the Fox and Hounds and the Carden Arms. Go straight forward in the direction of Shocklach and Worthenbury and have a look at the old stocks on the left. Pass the post office and the primary school. Shortly, Tilston church comes into view. Follow the lane as it winds its way to the church. Enter the church confines. The origins of the church date back to the 14th century and the ancient custom of rush-bearing still continues; so does the annual Wakes festival during which the first slice from an ox-roast is auctioned to the highest bidder.

Leave the church grounds at the rear, through a small wooden kissing gate. Turn left and cross a brook via a small footbridge. Turn right and proceed, keeping a hedge and trees on your immediate left. Shortly, the hedge turns away to the left, but keep forward here and cross a large facing field. On reaching overhead power lines bear diagonally left to follow the route of the power lines. Go over a stile which is set in a fence between 2 oak trees. Cross a field, still following the route of the power lines, then pass through a field gate. Turn left and immediately pass through a second gate to walk along a fenced-in track. The track descends and takes you onto a crossing lane via a couple of gates. Turn right, then almost immediately left to cross over a stream via a stone footbridge.

The area around here is still part of the sprawling village of Tilston, and when I passed this way there was an interesting antiques shop close to the footbridge.

On crossing the footbridge turn left and climb. Pass Hill Top and continue along the lane. Shortly, the lane goes over a stream then climbs to join a crossing lane close to cottages. Turn right now and follow the lane past a track which goes off to the left. Follow the lane for almost ½ mile, to where, on the left, a footpath sign indicates Higher Carden. The footpath is hedged-in and leads to a facing field gate. Go through the gate and enter a long field. Proceed along the right-hand edge of the field. Go through a field gate at the far corner of the field and continue in the same general direction as before. Walk towards another gate which comes into view straight ahead. On passing through this gate, turn left and follow a hedged-in track. The track turns right and leads to a gate. Pass through this gate and join a crossing lane where the way is left. Climb steadily to arrive at a T-junction in the tiny village of Higher Carden. Turn right here, and follow a lane which weaves around the base of Carden Cliff, a wooded hillock on the right.

Over to the left there are extensive views across to the Welsh hills. The lane takes you back to the car, which is parked ½ mile away.

WRENBURY

★

6 miles (9.5 km)

OS Landranger 117 and 118

The Dusty Miller Inn is situated by the Shropshire Union Canal ¼ mile from the centre of Wrenbury village. There is a counterbalanced road bridge across the canal here. Drive away from this bridge in the direction of Wrenbury Frith and Cholmondeley. After 180 metres the road crosses the river Weaver. Park the car at the side of the road here, where there is good verge parking available. (Map ref. 588 481).

On leaving the car, walk back along the road and cross the canal via the counterbalanced road bridge. Keep forward past the Dusty Miller and Cotton Arms Inns to arrive at Wrenbury village green. The 3-cornered green is surrounded by houses, all of which have neat, well-tended gardens. On the left stands the fine 16th century St Margaret's church. The church contains a monument dedicated to the memory of Sir Stapleton Cotton, who was a friend and fellow soldier of Wellington. He played a leading part in the victory of Salamanca, for which he was made a viscount, taking the name Combermere, from his family home, Combermere Abbey, which stands to the south of Wrenbury.

About 100 metres after passing the church turn left, to enter a narrow macadam drive between houses. There is a footpath sign here. Pass over a stile at the side of a facing gate and continue along a hedged-in track. Emerge from this track and go over a stile which is set in a fence on the left. Walk along a field edge, in the same general direction as before, keeping a hedge and fence on your immediate left. Go over a stile at the field corner. Cross 2 further stiles and arrive at a small hump-backed bridge which leads over the Shropshire Union Canal. Cross the bridge, go over a fence, then bear right to cross over rough terrain. On meeting the corner of a barbed-wire fence keep to the right and walk forward with a barbed-wire fence on your immediate left. Go over a facing stile which is near to a field gate. Turn left. Straight ahead can be seen the fine old building of Wrenbury Hall. Walk forward aiming to the right of the hall and cross a field in the direction of houses which can be seen straight ahead. Emerge from the field through a gate which is set between the houses.

On the left there is an entrance drive and no-entry sign, but keep forward along a facing lane. After 150 metres go over a stile on the right which is at the side of a field gate. Turn left and then right to follow a field edge and after 120 metres go over a stile on the left at the field

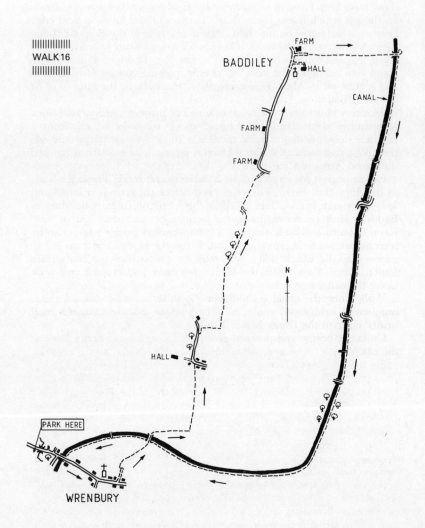

||||||||||||
WALK 16
||||||||||||

FARM

BADDILEY

HALL

CANAL

FARM

FARM

N

HALL

PARK HERE

WRENBURY

54

corner. Keep forward now with a hedge and trees on the immediate right. Go over a stile at the field corner. Bear slightly right now and walk past a row of trees which are set in a large field. After passing these trees keep forward to arrive at the field corner. Go through a gate on the left which leads over a dyke. Turn right and follow a field edge keeping a hedgerow on the right. Pass over a stile at the side of a facing gate. A short stretch of track takes you onto a crossing lane via a stile. Turn left and follow the lane as it winds past Baddiley Hulse Farm. Keep forward along the lane for ½ mile, passing Norton House Farm and a turn-off to Mere House en route, to arrive at the church of St Michael, Baddiley.

This tiny church is of medieval origin. The present building is of brick and timber construction and has 2 mock windows which, from a distance, look genuine. Inside there is a small 3-tiered pulpit and old pews, together with an unusual chancel screen, above which is painted the Royal Arms of Charles II.

Continue past the church along a facing gravel track. The track leads to Baddiley Hall Farm. Turn right just before the farm is reached and follow a rough track. Over to the right is the old manor building of Baddiley Hall. Go through a pair of facing gates and enter a large field. Keep forward and walk towards a hump-backed bridge which can be seen across the field, straight ahead. Cross the bridge and turn left to go over a stile which takes you onto the towpath of the Shropshire Union Canal. Pass under the bridge you have just crossed and walk along the canal towpath.

Walk along the canal towpath for 2½ miles, passing 3 locks and a number of bridges en route, to arrive at the counterbalanced road bridge close to the Dusty Miller Inn.

Cross the bridge and proceed down the facing lane to arrive back at the car.

TUSHINGHAM

WALK 17

★

3 miles (5 km)

OS Landranger 117

Tushingham sits amidst the lush green countryside close by the Shropshire border. It lies close to the Shropshire Union Canal and has 2 fine churches, one 200 years older tnan the other.

The A41 road connects No Man's Heath with Grindley Brook. Midway between these 2 places, and lying just off the main road, is the Blue Bell Inn. Drive past the inn and park the car ½ mile farther on, on the left, where there is a parking area opposite a school. (Map ref. 522 461).

On leaving the car, walk forward, cross the main road, and turn left to follow the roadside footpath in the direction of the church which can be seen straight ahead. Turn right just before the church and pass through a metal kissing gate. After 60 metres pass through a second kissing gate and keep forward along a field edge. After a further 80 metres go through a third kissing gate and enter a large field. Bear diagonally right now and go over a stile at the field corner.

You have now joined the Sandstone Trail, a continuous footpath running from Frodsham to Whitchurch. (A fair proportion of the trail is covered by a series of circular walks in Cheshire Walks for Motorists). The trail is identified by way markers—small wooden squares engraved with a footprint containing the letter S, together with a directional arrow.

Across the field straight ahead, can be seen the church of 'Old St Chad'. This tiny brick church was erected in 1689 and has hardly changed since the day it was built. Services are still held in the church, but only infrequently. Follow the Sandstone Trail as it passes to the right of the church over a stile where a sign points towards Grindley Brook.

Follow the Sandstone Trail for 1 mile, keeping a careful eye open for the way-markers, to arrive at Willeymoor Lock on the Shropshire Union Canal. An interesting 5 minutes can be spent here, watching the canal boats as they pass through the lock.

Leave the lock via the stile by which you arrived and walk forward to go over a fence-stile in a fence on the left. Enter a field and bear right to walk across the field, keeping to the right of a telegraph pole. Go over a stile, and keep forward across a field in the direction of a bungalow which can be seen straight ahead. A stile takes you onto a

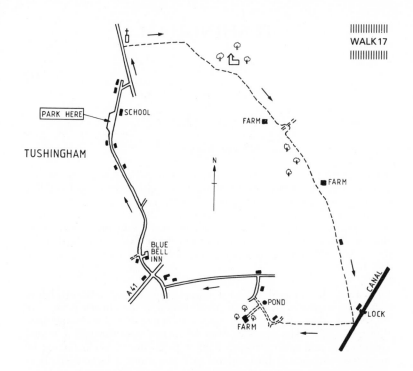

track in front of the bungalow. Follow the track as it turns to the right and keep forward past a turnoff to the left. The way now has a rough macadam surface and leads past a farm entrance drive on the left, which is opposite a small pond. Arrive at a T-junction. Turn right and follow a lane. Pass a dwelling on the right and shortly arrive at a T-junction where there is a facing cottage with a small wooden barn at its right-hand side. The lane to the right leads to Willeymoor, but turn left and climb along the lane. The lane reaches more level terrain and leads to a T-junction close to a bungalow and farm outbuildings on the right. Turn right. After 80 metres cross the main road and proceed past the Blue Bell Inn.

Continue for a further ½ mile, to arrive back at the car which is parked on the left.

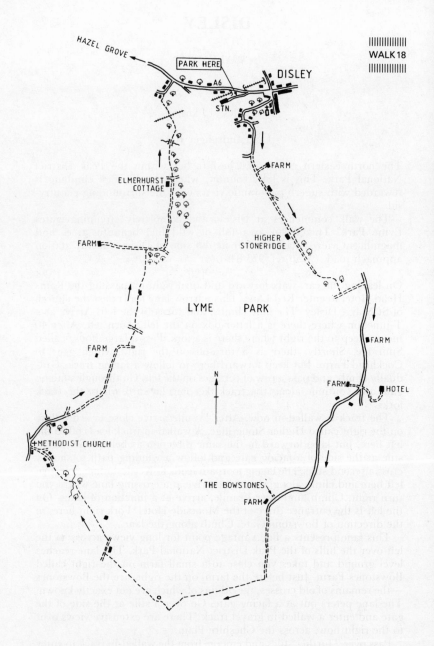

HAZEL GROVE

PARK HERE

DISLEY

A6

STN.

FARM

ELMERHURST
COTTAGE

FARM

HIGHER
STONERIDGE

LYME   PARK

FARM

FARM

N

FARM

FARM   HOTEL

METHODIST CHURCH

THE BOWSTONES

FARM

|||||||||||
WALK 18
|||||||||||

DISLEY

WALK 18

★

8 miles (13 km)

OS Landranger 109

The north eastern corner of Cheshire lies within the Peak District National Park. This is hilly country, where the effort of climbing is rewarded with superb panoramic views over the surrounding countryside.

The walk commences at Disley, and completely circumnavigates Lyme Park. This is an area full of wild life, beautiful trees and magnificent views. Park the car at the side of Disley railway station approach road. (Map ref. 973 846).

On leaving the car, walk forward and turn right on passing the Rams Head Hotel to enter Red Lane. This narrow lane leads past the church of St Mary, Disley. The lane climbs, and turns to the left. Arrive at a T-junction where there is a letter-box on the left. Turn left. After 40 metres keep to the right where there is a fork. Pass a large house called Sunridge. Shortly, there is a turn-off on the right which goes to Cockhead Farm, but keep forward here to follow a facing track. Gradually climb, and pass a row of cottages on the left. Go through a facing gate and continue along the track, keeping forward where the track forks.

The track is walled-in now. After ¼ mile arrive close to a dwelling on the right called Higher Stoneridge. A walled-in track leads off to the left here, but keep forward in the same direction as before. Go over a stile at the side of a facing gate and follow a winding path to shortly cross a second stile. The facing footpath leads to Kettleshulme, but turn left here and climb along a track to arrive at a crossing lane where you turn right. Climb, and after ½ mile, arrive at a junction of lanes. On the left is the entrance drive of the Moorside Hotel. Fork right here, in the direction of Bowstone Gate. Climb along the lane.

This lane presents a fine vantage point for long views across to the left over the hills of the Peak District National Park. The lane reaches level ground and takes you close to a small farm on the right called Bowstones Farm. Just before the farm, on the right, are the Bowstones —the remains of old crosses, the origins of which are not exactly known. The lane peters out at a facing gate. Go over a stile at the side of the gate and enter a walled-in gravel track. There are extensive views over to the right now, across the Cheshire Plain.

Pass over 2 further stiles and emerge from the walled-in track to enter a rough, moorland area. Turn right here, and proceed with a dry stone wall on your immediate right. After 150 metres cross a fence and continue along an undulating track which hugs the wall on the right. After ½ mile, the track gradually bears to the left away from the wall. Continue along the track, but after a further 250 metres turn right and follow a slightly raised grassy track which leads back towards the wall on the right. After 50 metres climb up a bank on the left and walk to the left of a low sunken pit which resembles a tiny volcano. Go over a stile in a crossing fence; this stile is about 60 metres away from the wall on the right. Walk forward now and descend, keeping a wall on your immediate right.

Descend for ½ mile, where once again there are superb views across the surrounding countryside. The path meets a crossing track close to a dwelling on the right. Turn right and walk past the dwelling, which is called Keepers Cottage. After 100 metres go over a stone stile on the left where a footpath sign indicates Higher Poynton. Bear slightly right and follow a well-worn path across a rough field. There is a dwelling over to the right. Follow a facing grassy path. The path descends shortly, then leads along the right-hand side of a narrow gorse-lined gully. Go over a stream via a rock bed, then continue with a wall on your immediate right. After 200 metres go through a gap in a crossing wall.

Proceed, and gradually descend, still keeping a wall on your immediate right. The wall on the right finishes. The path bears left now, then leads over more level ground to a facing gate where there is a dwelling set on higher ground at its rear. Go over a small stone stile at the left-hand side of the gate, then enter a facing track. There is a private gate on the right here, but keep forward along the facing gravel track. The track descends to a crossing lane close to the Methodist Church of Green Close, Pott Shrigley. Turn right, then right again, to enter a macadam drive between fences where a sign indicates Green Farm. The drive takes you over a stream and past a lodge-type dwelling on the right, and climbs to a facing gate. There is a turn-off to the left here, headed by a cattle grid, but keep forward and go over a large step-stile which is at the side of the gate.

Climb along a facing grassy track. Follow the track as it bears to the left. The track reaches more level ground and leads to a large kissing gate. There is a farm 250 metres away down on the left here. Follow the track as it gently bears to the right and arrive at a facing gate. Do not go through this gate but turn left and walk across a rough undulating area to arrive at a crossing track. Go over a facing step-stile which traverses a stone wall close to a gateway. Enter a large undulating field. Keep forward with a dry stone wall on your immediate right. Cross a wooden stile at the field corner, where there is a farm outbuilding on the right. Continue along a field edge with a wall still on your right, then go over a stone stile at the field corner. Walk forward, then descend to arrive at a crossing track. Turn right and pass over a cattle grid.

After 120 metres the track forks. Keep left and walk along a semi-macadamed track as it bends to the left.

There is a tall square stone tower on top of a hill on the right. This tower is known locally as 'The Cage' and is in the grounds of Lyme Park.

After ½ mile arrive close to a house on the left called Elmerhurst Cottage. Keep forward now and go over a facing stone stile where a signpost indicates High Lane and Marple. Descend along a field edge keeping a stone wall on your immediate right. Cross a small footbridge which leads over a stream then go over a stone stile in a facing crossing wall.

The path climbs and leads to railway lines. The way is forward across the railway lines, but be extremely careful here and look both ways before crossing, as the railway is in constant use. Go over a stone stile, then continue with a wall on your right. Cross a small wooden stile, then walk forward to join a facing lane close to a dwelling. Keep forward and climb to a crossing road. Turn right and follow the roadside pavement past the entrance drive of Lyme Park.

Keep forward now for ½ mile, to arrive back at Disley and the car.

POTT SHRIGLEY

WALK 19

★

7½ miles (12 km)

OS Landranger 109 and 118

The tiny village of Pott Shrigley nestles amongst the rolling foothills of the Peak District National Park. There are well-kept cottages here and an interesting church. There is some uphill walking involved, which is rewarded by magnificent views over the surrounding countryside.

The village of Adlington straddles the A523 road midway between Macclesfield and Hazel Grove. Leave the car on a roadside parking loop which is on the Hazel Grove side of the Legh Arms Hotel at the side of the A523 road. (Map ref. 912 806).

On leaving the car, walk past the front of the Legh Arms Hotel then turn left, to enter Brookledge Lane. Pass over the railway and keep forward past Legh Road. Turn next right along Wych Lane. Follow the lane past detached dwellings to arrive at Broughton Road, which is on the right. Keep forward here and enter a facing gravel track. The track gradually climbs. There is a wood on the right. About 200 metres after passing a secluded dwelling on the left, called Wych Cottage, the track turns sharply to the right. Leave the track here and go over a facing stile which leads into a field.

Keep forward with a hedge on the left at first, then on in the direction of farm buildings which come into view straight ahead. Walk to the right of a small pond and follow a track which leads to a facing gate close to farm outbuildings. Go over a stile at the side of the gate and keep forward to shortly cross a stile at the side of another gate. Some 20 metres farther on, go over a stile on the right which leads into a field. Climb up the facing field and after 200 metres go over a stile on the left, at the rear of a tall oak tree. Enter a large, undulating field. Bear diagonally left now, and after 150 metres walk close to a corner hedgerow which turns away to the left. Keep forward in the same direction as before, and climb towards trees. Bear right at the trees and climb. Pass over a pair of stiles which lead across a redundant railway line, then bear right and climb, keeping trees on your immediate left. After 200 metres go over a small bridge which takes you over the Macclesfield Canal. Follow a facing track to a crossing lane and turn right.

Pass dwellings on the right, then turn left to enter a gravel track. There is a footpath sign here, and other signs indicate Breck Farm, Little Breck and Breck Cottage. Follow the track, keeping forward

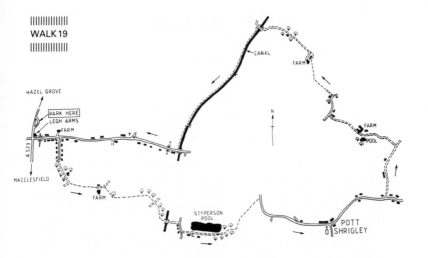

where it forks, and walk along the right-hand bank of Styperson Pool. This is a tranquil place, and there are many different species of birds to be seen in the area.

Keep forward where the pool on the left finishes, and follow a well-worn path through trees. Emerge from the trees and go over a facing stile. Walk forward now and gradually climb, with gorse bushes on either side, to follow a path which leads onto a crossing lane via a stile. There are long views looking back from here, across the Cheshire Plain.

Turn right and follow the lane as it gradually climbs and turns to the left. Keep forward past Long Lane, which leads off to the right. On the left shortly, can be seen the fine building of Shrigley Hall, which is now an hotel and country club. Follow the laneside pavement for ½ mile, and descend into the village of Pott Shrigley. There are neat, well-kept cottages on the left and the interesting church of St Christopher on the right.

Leave the village in the direction of Kettleshulme and Whaley Bridge. Follow the laneside pavement and climb past dwellings and Homestead Farm. Keep forward (there is no laneside pavement now) to enter a gravel track on the left, just before a works is reached. A sign at the head of the track indicates Heatherdale Farm. The track climbs at first, then reaches level ground and leads past a row of cottages on the left. Continue with a stone wall on your immediate left, pass a bungalow, and keep forward along a grassy track. Go over a stile at the side of a facing gate. About 100 metres farther on, turn left and enter a walled-in track which descends. There is a facing gate close to the head of this track. The track leads over a small stream where there is a pool on the left and a farm on the right. Go over a stone stile at the side of a gate and follow the track past large outbuildings. The track descends to a crossing lane. There is a row of charming cottages on the right here, called Cophurst Knott. Turn right along the lane. After 250 metres, enter a track on the left which commences between stone posts. There is a footpath sign here which indicates Poynton.

A hedged-in track leads to a facing field gate. Go through a gap at the side of this gate and continue along the left-hand side of a large field, keeping a hedge on your left. After 100 metres bear diagonally right and cross the field aiming to the right-hand side of a farm which can be seen straight ahead. Cross a stile close to the farm outbuildings. Keep forward and quickly cross a second stile on the left where the outbuildings finish. Walk forward and almost immediately cross another stile, which leads into a hedged-in lane.

Keep forward now and follow the lane for almost ½ mile, to arrive at a stone bridge which leads over the Macclesfield Canal. Cross the bridge and turn left to descend steps which lead onto the canal tow-path. Follow the tow-path away from the bridge.

Keep forward along the canal tow-path for 1 mile, and pass under bridges 19 and 20 to arrive at bridge 21. Walk under bridge 21, then leave the tow-path to the right. Climb to a crossing lane and turn left to follow the lane away from the bridge.

Walk past a neat row of cottages on the left and follow the lane over the redundant railway. Pass Poundy Lane, which is on the right, and keep forward past St John's Church, Adlington, and a school.

Follow the roadside pavement for almost 1 mile, to arrive back at the A523 road, close to where the car is parked.

BIRTLES

WALK 20

★

5 miles (8 km)

OS Landranger 118

The tree-clad hill at Alderley Edge is a notable view-point for extensive views over Cheshire and Lancashire.

The walk commences from a large public car park which is situated just off the B5087 road close to the Wizard Inn. (Map ref. 860 772). Legend tells that the inn lies close to a cave where, many years ago, a local man was taken by a wizard. The outcome of his visit is lost in time, but people are always claiming to have seen the wizard—so keep a sharp eye open on this walk.

Leave the car park via the main entrance. Turn left, and then right to enter a lane which is headed by a sign indicating 'Bradford Lodge Nurseries'. After 200 metres turn left at a T-junction. The lane turns to the left after ¼ mile, but keep forward here to go over a facing stile. The path leads straight across a field, then continues with a hedge on the right. Cross a couple of stiles, then emerge onto a crossing lane. Turn right and climb slightly at first, then descend to arrive at cross-roads. Keep forward here and enter a facing track which commences at the right hand side of a post box. The track leads past Jarmans Farm. Keep forward, then go through a facing gate at the side of a dwelling. There is a farm on the left now, but keep forward and gradually descend along a facing macadam lane. Go over a cattle grid and follow the lane for ¼ mile to arrive at a T-junction.

The way is left now, but first of all have a look at the tiny church of St Catherine's, Birtles, which is on the right. The church has an octagonal tower and contains many fine carvings. The old glasswork let into the more modern fabric is mainly the work of Flemish craftsmen.

On leaving the church, turn left as directed and follow the lane as it gradually climbs up a facing hill. After ¼ mile turn right and enter the entrance drive of Highlees Farm. The drive shortly descends through trees. The facing drive climbs towards the farm, which can be seen sitting on a rise straight ahead; do not climb towards the farm, but cross a stile on the left at the side of a large tree. The path runs along the edge of a field where there is a fence, and trees, on the immediate left. About 250 metres farther on, turn right at facing trees. Climb, keeping a fence, and the trees, on your immediate left. Go over a stile which leads onto a rough, gravel track where the way is left.

This is a pleasant place. The secluded valley on your right abounds

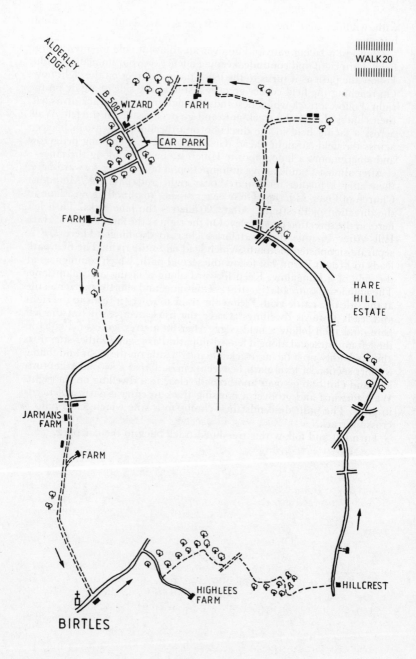

ALDERLEY
EDGE

B 5087

WIZARD

FARM

CAR PARK

FARM

HARE
HILL
ESTATE

N

JARMANS
FARM

FARM

HIGHLEES
FARM

HILLCREST

BIRTLES

with wildlife, and the facing earth banks are riddled with rabbit burrows.

Climb to a facing gate and go over an adjacent stile to enter a large field. Turn right and continue, keeping a fence on your immediate right. Follow the path as it turns to the left—there are trees on the right now. On reaching the field corner go over a stile at the side of a gate on the right. Follow a track which descends through trees. The track turns left, then climbs. Leave the track now and go over a stile on the left. Walk across a facing field in the direction of a dwelling which can be seen across the field, straight ahead. Go over a stile in a crossing hedgerow and emerge onto a lane opposite Hillcrest. Turn left along the lane.

After almost ½ mile arrive at a junction of lanes. Keep forward here, then after a further 350 metres bear right and pass the Methodist Church of Over Alderley. Go over a crossing road and enter a lane in the direction of Prestbury. After 200 metres the lane forks. Turn left here, in the direction of Alderley. On the right is the large estate of Hare Hill. After ½ mile the road forks, close to dwellings. There are 2, separate signposted footpaths which lead off to the right. The first path leads to Mount Farm, but follow the second path, which commences at the side of a bungalow. Keep forward along a facing macadam lane. The lane leads onto a facing track. Continue, and shortly go over a stile at the side of a cattle grid. Follow the track to where it turns to the right and leads towards dwellings. Leave the track over a stile on the left here, and then follow a field edge. After 80 metres, go over a stile on the left and descend along a fenced-in path. Pass over another stile then climb steadily up a facing track. Go over a stile on the right and follow a short section of level path between fences. Cross a second stile, turn left, and climb to go over another stile close to a dwelling on the right. Walk forward and go over a crossing track to enter a narrow, fenced-in path. The path descends then climbs to a stile which leads onto a crossing track.

Turn left and follow this tree-lined track back to the car park.

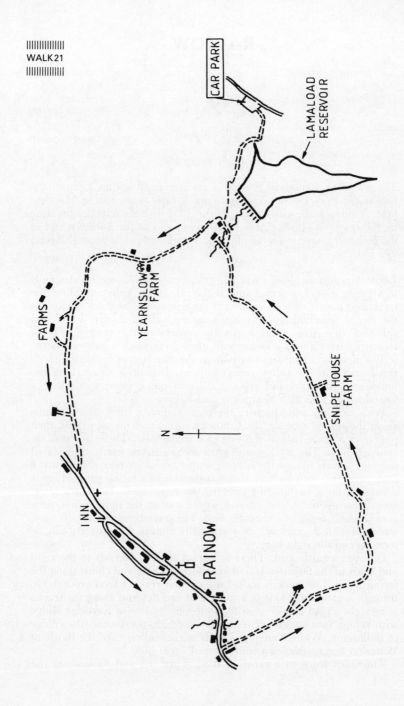

CAR PARK

LAMALOAD
RESERVOIR

FARMS

YEARNSLOW
FARM

N

SNIPE HOUSE
FARM

INN

RAINOW

RAINOW

WALK 21

★

5 miles (8 km)

OS Landranger 118

The waters of Lamaload Reservoir are contained within a dip in the hills of the Peak District National Park 4 miles to the east of Maccles-field. A minor road, which connects the A537 with the A5002, runs close by the reservoir. Just off this minor road, and at the northern end of the reservoir, there is a large official car park and picnic area. (Map ref 976 753).

Leave the car park along a winding gravel track which quickly descends to a facing gate. Go over a stile at the side of the gate and follow the track as it passes close to an inlet of the reservoir. The track climbs. At the top of the climb go over a stile at the side of a gate. There is a splendid view from here across the waters of the reservoir. Walk forward, turn right at a facing wall, then go through a gateway in the wall to descend along a grassy path in the direction of buildings which can be seen in the valley straight ahead. Just prior to reaching the buildings turn right and cross 2 stiles in quick succession where a footpath sign indicates Yearnslow and Rainow.
 Walk forward and climb to the right to join a track which climbs along the side of a facing hill. Continue with a wall on your right, then pass over a stone stile at the side of a facing gate. There is a wall on your left now. The track passes close to Yearnslow Farm, an isolated dwelling which sits on the hillside with trees at its rear. Climb away from the farm, then go over a stile at the side of a facing gate. There is a ruinous farm outbuilding over to the right here. The track leads forward across more level ground, with a wall on the right at first, then goes through a gap in a crossing wall. The track bends to the left now, leads through a gateway, then gradually climbs. Farmsteads can be seen over to the right here.
 Go over a cattle grid. There is a track which descends to the right and leads to the farmsteads, but keep forward here and climb along the facing track. The track is walled-in now and reaches level ground. Go through a gate at the side of a cattle grid and descend along the track.
 Straight ahead can be seen the mile-long outline of Kerridge Ridge with White Nancy standing at its right-hand end overlooking the village of Bollington. White Nancy was built in remembrance of the Battle of Waterloo and resembles a whitewashed sugar loaf.
 The track leads to a crossing road. Turn left and walk along the

69

roadside pavement. Follow the road as it descends into the village of Rainow. Pass the Robin Hood Inn. The roadside pavement ends shortly, so as a safer alternative, walk along Stocks Lane to rejoin the main road further on. Pass the parish church and at the bottom of the descent follow the road over a bridge which crosses the infant river Dean. The river, which begins its journey as an outlet from Lamaload Reservoir, meanders through Bollington and Handforth prior to its confluence with the river Bollin near Wilmslow.

Although Rainow stretches over many miles, it is in this immediate area that the nucleus of a village centre exists. The village contains many charming cottages which intermingle with more modern dwellings.

Climb past the war memorial and turn at the next left to enter a narrow lane where a footpath sign points towards the Gritstone Trail. Pass a row of cottages and go through a gate at the side of a cattle grid. Follow the lane as it climbs and bends past a number of dwellings. After 1 mile arrive close to a dwelling on the right called Snipe House Farm. There is a track which goes off to the right here, but keep forward to go through a gate at the side of a facing cattle grid and continue along the lane. Gradually climb, then follow the lane as it descends. The lane descends more steeply and turns to the right where Lamaload Dam can be seen straight ahead. The lane leads to a bridge close to waterboard property. Turn right just before this bridge and follow a footpath which leads to a facing gate. Go over a stile at the right-hand side of the gate and walk forward for 60 metres keeping a wall on your immediate left. Turn right now and climb along a way-marked footpath.

You are now back on part of the original route. Climb up the facing hill and retrace your original route back to the car park.

CAPESTHORNE

WALK 22

★

8 miles (13 km)

OS Landranger 118

A mixture of field paths, lanes, and old country tracks coupled with extensive views across the surrounding countryside combine to make this walk full of interest.

The A537 road connects Knutsford with Macclesfield. Three miles to the south of Alderley Edge the road runs between a roundabout at Chelford and traffic lights at Monk's Heath. Mid-way between these 2 places there is a roadside lay-by. Park the car here. (Map ref. 829 743).

On leaving the car, walk in the direction of Monk's Heath, using the roadside footpath. About 200 metres after leaving the car, turn right and cross the road to enter a narrow lane. A footpath sign here indicates Siddington and another sign Astle Farms. The lane leads to the tiny hamlet of Astle. Pass Astle Farm which is on the left. The lane shortly turns to the right where a sign indicates Astle Farm (west). Do not follow the lane as it turns to the right, but turn left, and go over a stile which leads into a field. Keep forward along the field edge for 80 metres then turn right (there is a footpath sign here). Continue, and after 100 metres go over a facing stile. Keep forward, passing to the left of 2 isolated trees, then gradually descend to go over a stile in a crossing fence. Pass to the right of a pond and quickly cross a second stile to enter a large field.

Keep forward bearing slightly left and descend towards facing trees. Cross a stream via a small bridge and stile. Go over a second stile which takes you into a field. Climb to the right, then keeping a low sunken wooded area on your left, cross a stile which is set close to a large oak tree. Keep forward now with a hedge on the right and walk in the direction of a small farm, which can be seen straight ahead. Join a gravel track and go through a facing gate. Pass to the right of the farm and follow the track to emerge at a bend in a crossing lane. Keep forward along the facing lane, passing dwellings on the left. After ¼ mile arrive at a small bungalow on the left. Go through a gate at the right-hand side of the bungalow and walk forward along a facing track, keeping trees and a fence on the left. A grassy track takes you to a large stone footbridge which traverses a lake, set in the gardens of Capesthorne Hall. Just before the bridge is reached, the hall comes into view across the lake on the left.

This magnificent house is ideally situated, and its tall towers and

71

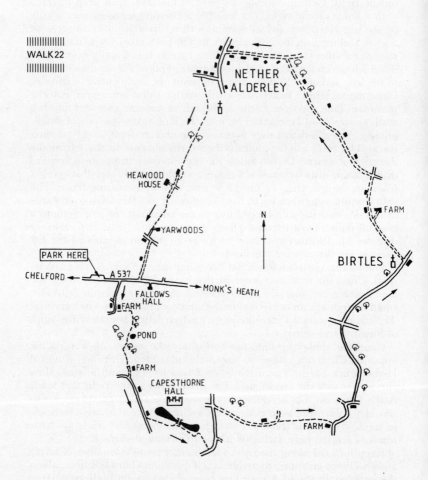

turrets look out over a glorious setting of woods and lakes. We are very fortunate indeed to have a public footpath passing so close to this superb mansion.

Do not cross the bridge, but go through a small metal kissing gate on the right. Continue along the edge of the lake, then keep forward with a fence on the right. On meeting a crossing fence go over a stile on the left. Keep forward for 40 metres then turn right to continue with a fence and trees on the immediate left. The path takes you to a crossing road via a stile. Cross the road, taking care as it is usually quite busy. Turn left and follow the roadside footpath. Follow the road as it bends to the left, and after ¼ mile, arrive opposite the main entrance drive of Capesthorne Hall. Leave the road to the right here, and enter a macadam lane. Go over a stile at the side of a facing gate and follow a straight stretch of lane. After ½ mile the lane takes you past a small-holding. Keep forward now over a cattle grid and out along a facing track. The track climbs slightly then turns sharply to the left in the direction of a farm. Do not follow the track to the left, but keep forward over a facing stile which is set close to a field gate. Proceed, keeping a fence on the left, then go over a second stile in a crossing fence. The way continues between earth banks and leads to a farm. Go over a stile at the side of a barn and pass close to the farmhouse to emerge onto a crossing lane. Turn left and climb along the lane. Pass the entrance drive of Marlheath Farm then arrive at a junction of lanes. Turn left here, in the direction of Chelford.

Follow this pleasant tree-lined lane for 1 mile, to arrive at a crossing road. Cross the road and enter Birtles Lane. Climb steadily along the lane for ¾ mile, to arrive at Birtles Church, which is on the left. This small church has an octagonal tower, and contains many fine carvings. The old glasswork let into the more modern fabric is mainly the work of Flemish craftsmen.

Continue along the lane for a further 100 metres, then turn left opposite Church Cottage to enter the macadam entrance drive of Higher Park Farm. The drive leads across level ground at first, then climbs towards the farmhouse. The drive turns to the right and leads to the farmyard, but keep forward now along a facing gravel track. Go through a gate and pass close to a dwelling. Proceed along a hedged-in track. The track takes you past Jarmans Farm and leads to cross-roads. Turn left here and walk along an old cobbled track.

Keep forward along the track for 1 mile, passing a number of farms and dwellings en route, to arrive at a T-junction. Turn left here, along the cobbled Bradford Lane. The lane gradually descends past large detached houses then meets a crossing road. Cross the road and turn left to follow the roadside footpath. Arrive at Sand Lane, which is on the right. Enter Sand Lane and after 200 metres leave the lane to the left, via a stile, where a footpath sign points to Alderley Church. The path dips and leads to a gate. There is a junction of paths here. The left-hand path leads directly to the church, but bear slightly right now to follow a path which leads towards trees.

73

Go over a stile and follow a path which winds for a short distance through trees. Pass over a second stile to enter a large field. Keep forward to follow the path as it crosses the field. Go over another stile near a gateway and continue across a second field. The path leads towards a dwelling which can be seen across the field straight ahead. Cross a combined footbridge and stile just before the dwelling, then turn left to follow a tall hedge as it turns to the right. The path takes you through a small wooden gate. Turn left now and follow a macadam drive. Pass in front of the entrance of Heawood House and 80 metres further on go over a stile at the left-hand side of a facing field gate. Enter a field and keep forward in the same general direction as before to cross a stile at the field corner. Proceed, keeping a fence on the immediate left. Pass over another stile and continue with a fence still on the left. Bear slightly right now and go over a stile which is set in a crossing hedgerow. Keep forward for 30 metres, with a hedgerow on your right, then pass over another stile which leads onto a facing macadam lane. To the left is a farm called Yarwoods, but keep forward along the facing lane. After 100 metres arrive at a T-junction where you turn left. After 40 metres turn right to enter a hedged-in track. Follow the track for ½ mile to arrive at a crossing road.

Turn right and walk back to the car, which is parked close by.

MACCLESFIELD FOREST

WALK 23

★

4½ miles (7 km)

OS Landranger 118

This walk leads from the wildlife sanctuary of Trentabank Reservoir and climbs to the isolated hilltop hamlet of Macclesfield Forest, which presents a fine vantage point for surveying the surrounding countryside.

The reservoirs of Ridgegate and Trentabank lie to the east of the village of Langley, and are some 3 miles to the south-east of Maccles-field. From Langley, drive in the direction of Macclesfield Forest. The lane climbs, then forks. Bear right here and drive along a lane which leads along the edge of Ridgegate Reservoir. On reaching the far end of the reservoir follow the lane as it bends to the left and arrive at Trentabank Reservoir, which is on the left. Park the car on the right where there is a public car park. (Map ref. 964 711).

On leaving the car park, turn right and walk along the lane. The way is forward to follow the lane as it climbs and winds through trees. You have an option shortly. You can follow a footpath which runs parallel to the lane and rejoins it after about 300 metres. This path is on the right and commences where a sign says, 'Standing Stone'. Just over ½ mile after leaving the car park turn off the lane and go over a stile at the side of a gate on the left. Walk forward along a gravel track through trees. The track quickly passes over a stream and narrows to become a gravel path. Climb between trees and, where the gravel finishes, pro-ceed along a facing grassy path. Continue, with a fence and a stone wall on the right, and climb to arrive at a crossing lane via a stile. Turn right and climb along the lane.

Over to the right there are superb views across to the wooded slopes of north-east Cheshire, where the summit of Shutlingsloe can be seen peeping out from behind the hills.

The lane leads into the tiny hamlet of Macclesfield Forest. The way is left now, along a rough stony track between stone walls where a sign says, 'Forest Walk'; however, before continuing, have a look at the simple little church of St Stephen's Macclesfield Forest. The original church was erected in 1673, but the present church was mostly rebuilt during 1834. The church has a small tower, and still celebrates a rush-bearing ceremony.

Climb along the track as directed and after 400 metres leave the track to the left where a sign says, 'Walker Barn 1½ miles'. Cross a stile and follow a well-worn path which leads into trees. Descend through quite

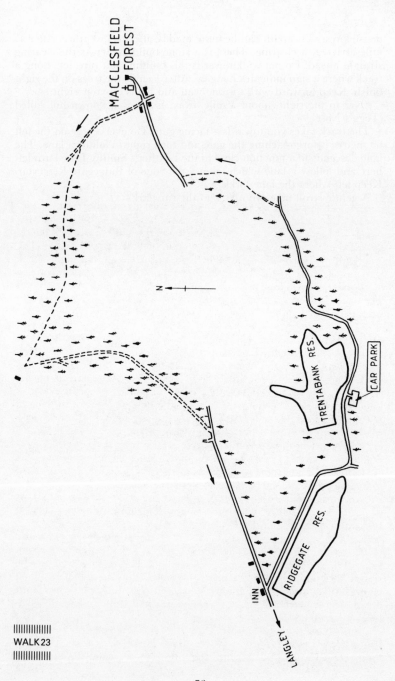

MACCLESFIELD
FOREST

TRENTABANK RES.

CAR PARK

RIDGEGATE RES.

INN

LANGLEY

N

WALK 23

dense forest. This path can be quite muddy after wet weather. After ¾ mile arrive at a clearing. There is a stone building across the clearing straight ahead. Do not walk towards this building but turn left along a track where a sign indicates Langley. After ½ mile the trees on the right finish. Keep forward with a stone wall and fields on your right.

Over to the right, about a mile away, is the well known hill called 'Tegg's Nose'.

The track takes you towards a facing gate. Go over a stile on the left 60 metres before reaching the gate and turn right to follow a lane. The lane descends to a junction close to the Leather's Smithy Inn. Turn left here and follow a lane which follows the edge of Ridgegate Reservoir. Keep left where the lane forks.

A gentle stroll takes you back to the car park.

GOOSTREY

WALK 24

★

5½ miles (9 km)

OS Landranger 118

This walk is easy going as it stays entirely on level ground. There are no stiles to negotiate and no cross-country footpaths to follow; the route being by way of bridle tracks and country lanes.

A narrow winding lane connects Peover Heath with Goostrey. Midway between both villages lies the scattered hamlet of Barnshaw. The parking area is close to a junction of lanes where a road sign indicates Peover Heath, Blackden Heath, Goostrey, and Withington Green. There is also a footpath sign pointing down a hedged-in track which leads away from the parking area. (Map ref. 782 719).

On leaving the car, enter the hedged-in track. Follow this leafy by-way, and after ½ mile pass a footpath which leads off to the right. Walk forward now past farm buildings and continue along a facing track. Pass a bungalow and, on passing a second farm, keep forward along a narrow macadam lane. The lane leads past another farm, followed by a house. On reaching a row of tiny cottages on the right, turn left and enter Booth Bed Lane.

Follow Booth Bed Lane for 1½ miles, passing a number of farms, and Brick Bank Lane en route. Shortly after passing a row of modern houses turn left and enter Sandy Lane. Keep forward past Swanwick Close, then follow a rough road to arrive at a T-junction. Turn left, and follow the roadside pavement into the village of Goostrey. The village is mostly modern, a fair amount of building having taken place in recent years, but nevertheless a lot of the 'old' atmosphere is still retained.

Follow the road through the village centre and pass the Crown Inn. Arrive at St Luke's Church. This pleasing building has a simple interior and 2 graveyards, one of which is across the road from the church confines. Keep forward now along Station Road and pass the Red Lion Inn, followed by a row of old cottages on the right. Turn left now and enter a gravel track where a footpath sign points away from the road. The track follows the edge of a large field, where Jodrell Bank radiotele-scope comes into view straight ahead. After ½ mile the track takes you past Blackden Hall, then bends to the left.

About ¼ mile farther on, pass close to a small cottage on the right, then keep forward, past dwellings on the left. Go straight over a crossing lane and follow a grassy track for 100 metres to a T-junction. Turn right and follow a lane for 80 metres to arrive at crossroads. Turn left then,

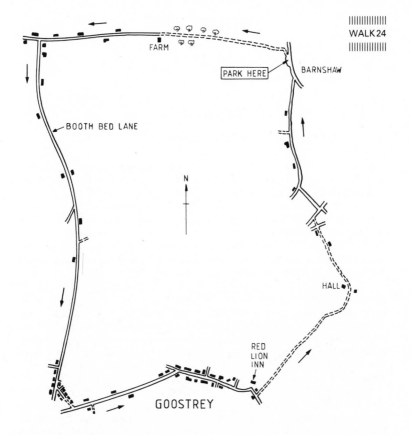

after ¼ mile, arrive at a T-junction. Turn right here, in the direction of Peover Heath. The lane leads past Blackden Heath Farm and the entrance drive of Barnshaw Hall Farm.

Shortly after passing Brookside Cottages arrive at a junction of lanes close to where the car is parked.

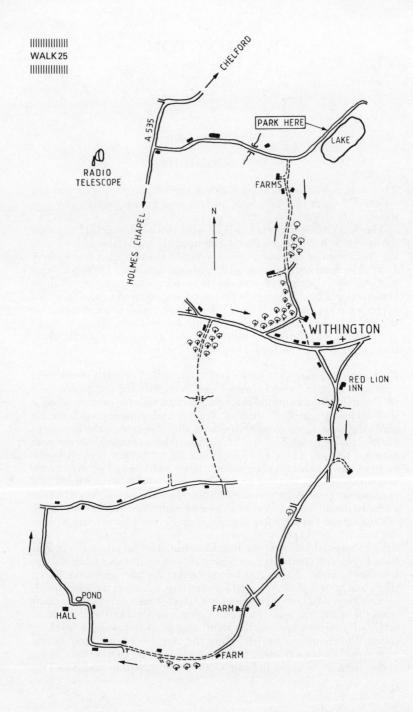

WALK 25

CHELFORD

A 535

RADIO
TELESCOPE

HOLMES CHAPEL

N

PARK HERE

LAKE

FARMS

WITHINGTON

RED LION
INN

POND

HALL

FARM

FARM

WITHINGTON

WALK 25

★

6½ miles (10.5 km)

OS Landranger 118

This walk will take you along winding lanes through the rich farming country of south-east Cheshire, an area well known for its dairy produce.

The A535 road connects Chelford with Holmes Chapel. Half a mile to the east of Jodrell Bank Radio Telescope there is a lane which leaves the A535 road in an easterly direction; this lane is called Catchpenny Lane. The head of the lane faces a road sign indicating Holmes Chapel and Alderley Edge, and is close to a telephone box. Drive along Catchpenny Lane, passing dwellings on left and right. The lane traverses a stream via a small bridge. Drive past Brook Farm, which is on the left, and the entrance drive of Smiths Green Farm, which is on the right. Drive for a further ¼ mile, then park the car on the left, where there is good verge parking. (Map ref 812 714).

On leaving the car, walk back along the lane and turn left to enter the approach track of Smiths Green Farm. Walk forward and pass a farm on the right, then continue through a second farm to keep on along a well-defined track. Pass through 3 gates and emerge onto a facing macadam lane. Keep forward to where, after 200 metres, the lane turns sharply to the right. Bear left here, then right, to enter a narrow path between hedges. There is a dwelling over to the left here. After 60 metres cross a stile and enter a field. Keep forward and go over a stile which can be seen straight ahead. A narrow fenced-in path leads to a crossing road where the way is left. After 30 metres turn right and follow a lane in the direction of Swettenham and Somerford. This is the village of Withington. On the left is the village green, across which can be seen the tiny village chapel.

Keep forward and pass the Red Lion Inn. The lane passes over Red Lion Brook and continues past a farm entrance drive and small bungalow on the right. About 250 metres farther on, the lane forks. Keep right, and after 400 metres keep forward past a lane on the right which goes to Twemlow Green and Holmes Chapel. Pass a narrow lane which leads off to the left, and follow the facing lane for a further ¼ mile to arrive at a narrow lane on the right, shortly after passing a dwelling called Whitehouse on the left. Enter the lane on the right and shortly walk straight over a crossing road to continue along another lane. Signs at the head of this lane indicate Cross Lane, Chestnut and Ash Tree

Farms. Pass a bungalow on the left, and the entrance drive of Cross Lane Farm on the right. Pass close to Chestnut Farm and keep forward along a facing track which traverses a tree-lined ridge. The area around here is kept as a Nature Reserve.

The track takes you close to another farm. There is a joining track on the left here which descends through trees, but keep forward along level ground and follow the facing track. Go through a gate and continue past a small farmhouse. Keep forward along a macadam lane. Follow the lane as it turns to the right between farm outbuildings. The lane is straight for 250 metres then turns to the left. Follow the lane to the left, then bear right and descend past a pond on the right. Sitting on a rise on the left is the imposing building of Kermincham Hall. Follow the facing lane as it passes over a stream. Gradually climb for ¼ mile and emerge onto a crossing lane. Turn right.

Follow the lane for almost ¾ mile, passing dwellings on left and right, to arrive at a lane on the right which leads to Swettenham. Go through a field gate on the left here, which is set between holly bushes. Proceed along a field edge, keeping a fence and a row of trees on your immediate right. After 250 metres arrive at the field corner and go over a stile at the side of a field gate. Turn right and immediately left, to proceed along a field edge in the same direction as before, with a fence and a hedge on your right. On reaching the field corner go over another stile and continue across a large undulating field. Bear diagonally right and descend to cross a small footbridge which takes you over a stream. Climb forward and bear left to go over a stile at the side of a field-gate which is set in a crossing fence. Keep forward across a large field and head towards trees. Pass over a stile at the side of an old metal field gate and follow a facing track between trees. The track emerges onto a crossing road close by Lower Withington Parish Hall. Turn right and walk along the roadside pavement. After 400 metres turn left and enter a narrow lane. There are trees on the left here. After 200 metres follow the lane as it turns to the left.

You are now back on part of the original route. Keep forward along the facing lane and retrace your original route back to the car.

BRERETON

WALK 26

★

3¼ miles (5 km)

OS Landranger 118

This short walk will take you along secluded lanes, which meander past a handsome 15th century church and a fine 16th century hall.

Park the car by the A50 road, 2 miles to the south of Holmes Chapel, where there are lay-bys on both sides of the road. The more southerly lay-by is best, otherwise the main road has to be crossed on foot. (Map ref. 774 651).

On leaving the car, walk forward along the roadside verge. After 120 metres go over a stile which is set in a hedge on the left and enter a large field. Keep along the field edge. There is a dwelling on the right here. Bear gradually left now and go over a stile which is to the right hand side of a field gate. Turn left and walk along a track which leads towards farm buildings. Pass between the outbuildings and turn right to go through gates which lead onto a facing lane. Pass the rectory, which is a large house on the left, to arrive at a junction of lanes. Turn left and continue.

A rather splendid view appears shortly on the left, where Brereton Hall and St Oswald's Church are to be seen across a meadow. The hall, which is now used as a school, was erected during the 16th century, and is one of the finest examples of its kind in the area.

Walk forward and follow the lane as it passes over the river Croco. A private lane on the left leads to the hall, but keep forward now to arrive at the church entrance gate.

Before continuing your journey take a look in and around this interesting church. The church dates from 1190 but was completely re-built during the 15th century. It contains a monument which shows William Smethwick, who died in 1643, and his wife. A leaflet describing points of interest for visitors is available inside the church.

On leaving the church, continue in the same direction as before, and follow a gravel track. Go through a gate which is set close to a cattle grid. Shortly, a junction of tracks is met. Bear right and walk forward to go through a wooden gate at the left hand side of a house. Keep forward along the facing track, where there is a fine view across to rolling hills on the right. See if you can pick out the tower of Mow Cop on the extreme right. About 200 metres after passing the house, go over a stile at the side of a field gate on the left. Walk along the edge of a large field keeping a hedgerow on your immediate right. About 30

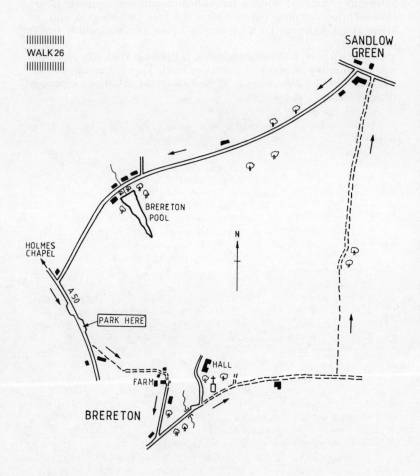

WALK 26

SANDLOW GREEN

BRERETON POOL

HOLMES CHAPEL

A 50

PARK HERE

HALL

FARM

BRERETON

N

metres before a crossing fence is arrived at, go over a stile at the side of a gate on the right. Proceed along a facing gravel track with a fence on the left at first, then with a fence on the left and a hedge on the right.

Follow the track for almost ½ mile and emerge onto a crossing road close to Sandlow Green Farm, where you turn left. After 60 metres turn left again to proceed down a lane which commences opposite Court House Farm—Sandlow Green. Follow the lane for almost ¾ mile, to arrive at a T-junction. Turn left here and pass dwellings which are on the right.

On the left here, half hidden by trees, is Brereton Pool. Keep forward now for ¼ mile and arrive at a crossing road. Turn left and follow the roadside verge for 350 metres to arrive back at the car, which is parked straight ahead.

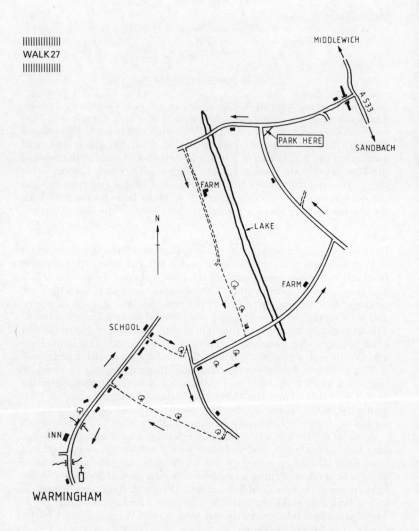

||||||||||||||
WALK 27
||||||||||||||

MIDDLEWICH

A 533

SANDBACH

PARK HERE

FARM

LAKE

FARM

N

SCHOOL

INN

WARMINGHAM

WARMINGHAM

WALK 27

★

4 miles (6.5 km)

OS Landranger 118

The charming village of Warmingham is set in a lush green hollow. There is a mill, a waterside inn, and a church, which dates from 1715.

The A533 road runs between Sandbach and Middlewich. Drive down Dragon's Lane, which commences 2 miles from Sandbach and runs away from the A533 road in a westerly direction. A sign at the head of the lane says, 'Axle Weight Limit 3 tonnes—No Track Laying Vehicles'. Cross the canal via a tiny hump-backed bridge and turn right at the next junction. After ¼ mile arrive at Plant Lane on the left. Park the car here, where there is a small parking area on the left. (Map ref. 724 623).

On leaving the car, walk forward along Dragon's Lane in the direction of Warmingham. Pass a small farm on the left and follow the lane as it descends to cross a long, narrow lake called Moston Flash which is a favourite haunt of local anglers. Keep forward and climb, then turn left to enter the entrance drive of Fields Farm, Moston. Follow the drive and walk on past the farmhouse. Keep forward along a fenced-in track. The fenced-in track turns to the right shortly, but keep forward here to enter a large field. Continue, keeping a hedgerow on your immediate left. Go through a gate at the field corner and continue with a hedgerow still on your left. Pass close to a dwelling, then emerge onto a crossing lane via a gate. Turn right and walk forward for 250 metres to arrive at a T-junction. Turn left. After 200 metres the lane begins to turn gently to the left. There is a dwelling on the left here. About 150 metres farther on, leave the lane to the right and follow a track between hedges.

After 50 metres go over a stile at the side of a field gate and enter a long field. Turn right, and continue with a tall hedge on the right at first. After 80 metres, go over a stile at the side of a gate, and continue along a field edge, keeping a hedgerow on your immediate right. At the field corner go over a double fence-stile. Proceed, then pass through a facing field gap and keep forward, still with a hedgerow on the right. There is a splendid view to the left now, where Warmingham Church can be seen across meadows.

The path continues through a field gap and follows a field edge to emerge onto a crossing lane through a pair of gates between dwellings. Turn left now and gently descend into Warmingham. There is a craft workshop and gallery on the right and to its rear a small museum of light aircraft has been established. Farther on, there is a mill, which has been modernised in recent years. The river Wheelock runs under the lane now. On the right is the Bears Paw Inn, whilst over a small bridge on the left is the church of St Leonard. The church tower dates from 1715 but the main fabric is more recent, and has replaced an earlier timber building. About 60 metres past the church there is a fine black and white farm building which has been restored to good effect.

Retrace your steps past the Bears Paw Inn, and climb away from the village centre. Follow the lane past the entrance drive of Warmingham Grange Country Club. Just before the village school, turn right and go over a fence-stile at the side of a field gate. Walk forward, between fences at first, then cross a rough field in the direction of a dwelling which can be seen straight ahead. Go over a fence-stile at the field corner then turn left along a field edge. Enter a crossing lane via a stile and turn right. After 100 metres turn left into Green Lane. (You walked along this section of lane earlier in the walk). Follow the lane as it passes over Moston Flash, then climb and pass a farm on the left. Arrive at a T-junction, where the way is left.

A short stroll of ¼ mile takes you back to the car.

BARTHOMLEY

WALK 28

★

4½ miles (7 km)

OS Landranger 118

The delightful village of Barthomley is set deep in the heart of south-east Cheshire. The village contains many lovely old black and white thatched cottages and boasts a handsome church, which has changed little during the last 400 years.

The parking location is a lay-by at the side of the A500 road to the western side of its intersection with the M6 motorway. If you are approaching the area along the motorway, leave at junction 16 and follow the A500 road in the direction of Crewe and Nantwich. Almost immediately you will arrive at a parking lay-by on the left-hand side of the road. (Map ref. 774 524).

On leaving the car, walk forward along the verge of the A500 road and after 200 metres ascend some steps which take you up a banking on the left. Cross a stile to enter a field. Turn right and shortly pass through a gate in a crossing hedge. Continue in the direction of a farm which can be seen 250 metres away straight ahead. The path leads into a hedged-in track which emerges onto a lane opposite Blue Mire Farm. Turn left and follow the lane into the village of Barthomley.

On the left is the White Lion Inn. The inn, which has a thatched roof, is beautifully preserved and dates from 1614. Facing steps lead into the church confines. The church has looked down on happy and troubled times. During the Civil War the village provided soldiers for the Parliamentarian forces. Shortly after the Battle of Nantwich marauding Royalist troops imprisoned a number of villagers in the church tower and then set fire to it. Many of the villagers perished during this most unpleasant episode. A leaflet describing points of interest is available inside the church.

Leave the village along a lane which leads between the White Lion Inn and the church confines. This lane is headed by a sign which points towards Audley. Follow the lane as it climbs and winds past farm and dwelling. After ½ mile the lane levels out, then descends past Knowl End Farm, which is on the left. About 100 metres farther on, there is a track which goes off to the right. Enter this track and almost immediately go over a stile on the right to enter a field. Turn left and gradually climb along the field edge, keeping a fence on your immediate left. Just before the field corner is reached go over a fence-stile on the left and descend to a crossing track. Turn right and pass to the right of

89

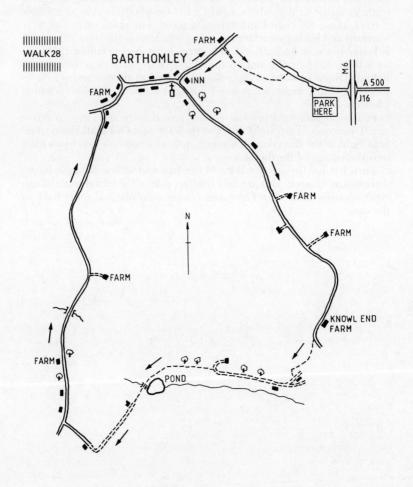

WALK 28

BARTHOMLEY

FARM
FARM
INN
FARM
FARM
FARM
FARM
FARM
KNOWL END FARM
POND

M 6
A 500
J 16
PARK HERE

N

a building and a dwelling to follow a track which takes you along a valley bottom, where there is a stream on your left. Follow the track for ¼ mile to where it turns to the right. The track climbs to a dwelling, but keep forward here to follow a path which runs along the side of a gorse and bramble covered banking. Shortly descend 3 steps and then pass over a fence-stile. Continue along the side of the banking. The path leads to a stile at the side of a field gate. Go over this stile and follow a track along the right-hand side of a pond. The track takes you over a stream and leads past a large dwelling which is on the right. The track is hedged-in now and after ¼ mile turns to the right. Follow the track as it turns to the right and go through a facing gate close to a small-holding. Keep forward along a macadam lane to shortly arrive at a T-junction. Turn right to proceed along a typical narrow, winding Cheshire lane.

Follow the lane for 1 mile as it winds past cottage and farm, to arrive at a T-junction. Turn right and shortly walk past Old Hall Farm, then bear right in the direction of Alsager. A short stroll now takes you back into the village of Barthomley.

Turn left just before the White Lion Inn and follow the lane in the direction of Alsager. You are now back on part of the initial route. Turn right opposite Blue Mire Farm and retrace your original route back to the car.

WYBUNBURY

WALK 29

★

3 miles (5 km)

OS Landranger 118

During this walk you will rarely lose sight of the tower of Wybunbury church. The tower, which dominates the surrounding countryside, has become a well-known Cheshire landmark.

The village of Hough lies on the A52 road mid-way between Nantwich and the M6 motorway. Drive due south away from the A52 road along Cobbs Lane. Pass Buck Lane, Rushton Drive and Pit Lane to arrive at Hough Common, which is on the left. There is a long narrow parking area on the left here. (Map ref. 715 506).

On leaving the car, walk back along Cobbs Lane for a short distance and fork left down Pit Lane. Keep forward past Woolston Drive and arrive at a T-junction. Turn left and walk along the verge at the side of the road. After 150 metres pass through a tall metal kissing gate on the left where a footpath sign indicates Wybunbury. Enter a large field and walk forward keeping a hedge on the left about 30 metres away. After 250 metres converge with the hedge on the left and walk forward to pass through a small metal kissing gate which is set in a crossing hedge. Enter a large field. Across the fields straight ahead can be seen the tower of Wybunbury Church.

Bear diagonally right, pass under telephone wires, then walk along the left-hand bank of a rectangular pond. Go over a facing stile. On the left here there is a low sunken wooded area. Keep forward aiming to the right of the church tower, pass through a hedge of trees, and descend to go over a stile at the right-hand side of a large tree. Keep forward along a well-worn path which shortly traverses a dyke via a double stile and concrete slab. Climb and pass through a facing kissing gate which leads into the church confines.

At the present time the tower stands alone, the main body of the church having been demolished. Earth movements had given the 15th century tower a pronounced 'lean' for which it was quite famous, but this misalignment has been virtually eliminated during recent years and it now stands on more solid foundations. The bulk of the village of Wybunbury lies to the right of the church through the main lych gate, and if time permits have a look around this interesting village.

Leave the church confines on the east side, through a wooden kissing gate, opposite the grave of Vera Stewart who died in 1989, aged 98 years. Descend steps made from old gravestones and pass through 2

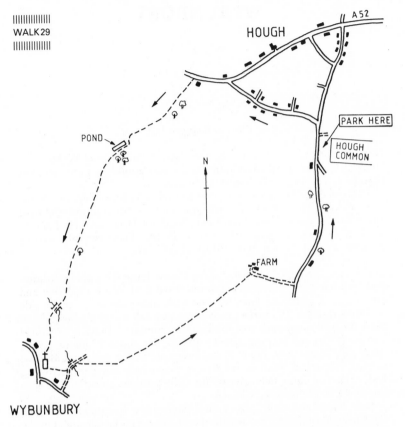

HOUGH

A 52

POND

N

PARK HERE

HOUGH COMMON

FARM

WYBUNBURY

kissing gates in quick succession to arrive at a crossing track. Turn left, cross a stream via a bridge, and immediately turn right through a field gate. Walk forward, bearing slightly right, and go over a stile in a crossing hedgerow. A farmhouse can be seen sitting on top of a rise straight ahead about ½ mile away. Walk in the direction of the farmhouse. Cross 2 fields and go over 2 stiles. Climb up towards the farm and go through a gate which takes you onto the farm entrance drive. A straight 300 metres along the farm entrance drive takes you onto a crossing lane. This is Cobbs Lane.

Turn left and follow the lane back to the car, which is parked on the right ½ mile away.

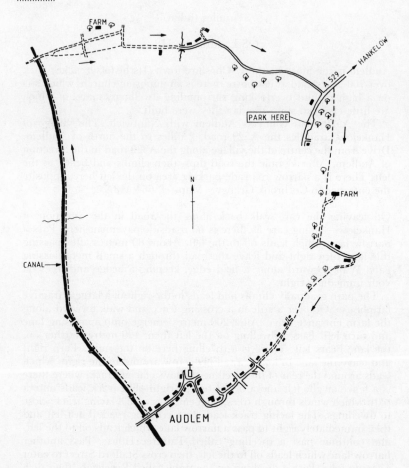

AUDLEM

WALK 30

★

3¾ miles (6 km)

OS Landranger 118

Audlem is the most southerly Cheshire town. Its history reaches back over 700 years, and at its centre there is an imposing church, which sits on a high mound overlooking surrounding dwellings, many of which are little changed since the day they were built.

The A529 road connects Audlem with Nantwich. The village of Hankelow straddles the A529 road, 2 miles to the north of Audlem. Drive from the centre of the village along the A529 road in the direction of Audlem. After ½ mile the road dips, then climbs and bends to the left. There is a narrow roadside parking area on the left here, opposite the entrance to Corbrook Grange. (Map ref. 664 448).

On leaving the car, walk back along the road in the direction of Hankelow—taking care as there is no roadside pavement here. Pass a narrow lane which leads off to the left. About 80 metres after passing this lane turn right and leave the road through a small metal kissing gate. Walk forward along a field edge, keeping a hedge and trees on your immediate right.

The path gradually climbs and leads to the right of a large attractive farmhouse. Go over a stile in a crossing fence and walk forward along the farm entrance drive. After 200 metres emerge onto a crossing lane and turn left. Pass a dwelling on the left then, 100 metres farther on, the lane bears left. There is a dwelling here on the right. Turn right and leave the lane to follow a tall hedgerow around to the right, which leads around the rear of the dwelling. Follow a facing track, where there is a fence on the left and a hedge on the right. The track leads onto a path which winds through trees, then emerges onto a facing track, close to dwellings. The facing track leads to a crossing road. Turn left and then immediately right to pass a narrow lane which leads off to the left, and continue past a dwelling called Taintree House. Pass another narrow lane which leads off to the left, then cross Stafford Street to enter a facing lane. Pass a dwelling on the right called Roseleigh, then turn next left on passing Brookside to enter a narrow lane. Pass Daisy Cottage and follow the lane as it gently turns to the right past the old grammar school. A tablet, which is set in the wall here, shows that the school was founded in 1655. The lane climbs and emerges onto a crossing road opposite the church of St James, Audlem.

The church, which dates from the 13th century, and sits on a high mound in the centre of this lovely little town, contains many items of interest. There is a medieval chest and 2 old fonts, one of which is said to have been carved before the Reformation. The lofty nave roof has been recently restored after a ravaging by death-watch beetle. The stained-glass windows are of excellent quality. Outside there is an old sundial, and a priests' doorway which is now too high for anyone to reach.

On leaving the church, follow the road in the direction of Whitchurch. Pass Audlem Methodist Church, which is on the left. Turn right on passing the Bridge Inn, and follow a lane which takes you onto the tow-path of the Shropshire Union Canal close to the Shroppie Fly Inn. There is a lock on the canal here. Keep forward along the tow-path and pass 2 further locks, to arrive at a bridge. Walk under the bridge and continue along the tow-path. Across the canal on the left are the old stable buildings of the Shropshire Union Canal Company, which are a reminder that horse-drawn barges were a familiar sight in this part of Cheshire up to the Second World War. The canal is raised above the level of the surrounding fields now, and there are fine views to left and right.

Keep along the tow-path for ¾ mile, to arrive at bridge No. 80. Walk under the bridge and turn right to leave the canal tow-path. Go through a gate at the side of the bridge and enter a hedged-in track. Turn left and follow the track away from the bridge. After 30 metres go through a facing gate. After a further 60 metres, the hedge on the right kinks to the right, where there is a field gate. Go through this gate. Turn left and proceed in the same general direction as before, gradually bearing right away from a fence on the left. Walk straight over a crossing track and go over a stile which is at the left-hand side of a facing gate.

Walk forward now along a field edge, keeping a fence on your immediate right. Go over a pair of stiles, and continue along a facing drive. Pass a dwelling on the right and descend. Cross over the infant river Weaver via a bridge and follow a facing lane which takes you past Hankelow Mill (now a private house). A mill has been on this site for over 300 years and part of the old workings can still be seen down by the riverside. Continue past The Riverside Mews. There is a dwelling sitting on top of a rise on the left now called Mill House. Follow the facing lane as it winds and climbs through trees, and after ½ mile emerge onto a crossing road.

Turn right and climb back to the car, which is parked on the left.